Also by Richard W. Langer

The After-Dinner Gardening Book
Grow It!
Grow It Indoors
The Joy of Camping
The Bread Machine Bakery Book
More Recipes for Your Bread Machine Bakery
Bread Machine Sweets and Treats
The Complete Bread Machine Bakery Book

by

RICHARD W. LANGER

Illustrations by Susan McNeill

Little, Brown and Company

BOSTON   NEW YORK   LONDON

WHERE THERE'S
SMOKE
THERE'S FLAVOR

WHERE THERE'S
SMOKE
THERE'S FLAVOR

Real Barbecue—
The Tastier Alternative to Grilling

Library of Congress Cataloging-in-Publication Data

Langer, Richard W.
    Where there's smoke there's flavor : real barbecue—the tastier alternative to grilling / Richard W. Langer.
        p.   cm.
    Includes index.
    ISBN 0-316-51301-6
    1. Cookery (Smoked foods)   I. Title
TX835.L36   1996
641.4′6—dc20   95-49916

Designed by Jeanne Abboud

10   9   8   7   6   5   4   3

MV-NY

PRINTED IN THE UNITED STATES OF AMERICA

To the Thanksgiving crowd —
long may we gather

CONTENTS

WHERE THERE'S
SMOKE
THERE'S FLAVOR

1. SMOKE COOKING, THE TRULY AMERICAN BARBECUE

It was on a dark and stormy October night some thirty years ago that I attended my first real barbecue. A number of reasons had contributed to my previous deprivation. For one thing, I'd done the early part of my growing up in Europe, where cooking outside over an open fire was simply not one of life's options. After all, mankind had spent centuries taming fire, reducing its presence from a sooty thing on an open hearth to a subdued flame impounded in an iron box brightly enameled to conceal all its grubby companions — smoke, ash, grit. Why would anyone want to release Prometheus once more — and in the garden, at that? Besides, cooking was women's work.

Suffused with that particular envy that afflicts someone raised on yellow-pea soup and herring and then transported to the land of hamburgers and roast beef, I eagerly anticipated the fifties and sixties backyard cookouts to which I was invited by new neighbors and friends in this country. I'm not quite sure what I expected. Certainly it was not the charred remains so often presented there upon a paper plate.

As I was to learn in due course, these repasts, called barbecues, were that in name only. True barbecuing was a country affair evolved in the time warp of the South, where an hour might last a day. The art is as compatible with the fifty-minute hour of the suburban Northeast as hominy grits are with Grey Poupon. Now, mind you, I don't care how grits are cooked. I can live quite well without that southern specialty. A good barbecue, however, I would find difficult to pass up, having discovered its merits. As a pacemaker for the soul in a computer-clocked world, a tastifier of foods, and a focus for gathered friends, it has few rivals.

So what is a barbecue, really? Well, it's time — time for curling, drifting smoke to flavor the food; time filled with talk; time to relax and enjoy the best of two worlds, the slower, simpler pace of yesterday and today's technological advances — for not all of them are to be eschewed. It's taking life easy, a gift we seem to have lost in our rush to work and the mall and back again. What it's not is the tossing of a burger or a chunk of steak onto a flaming backyard rack by what can only be called a culinary pyromaniac, there to burn black on the outside, remaining raw inside. That's grilling. Barbecue aficionados disparagingly refer to such a cookout as a "grill-e-Q."

Grilling, as defined by the famous French chef Auguste Escoffier a hundred-odd years ago, is essentially cooking food quickly over a hot fire. When food is exposed to the intense direct heat of flames, it acquires a seared, flavorsome crust. Depending on the technique and skill of the chef and the amount of grease feeding the Vesuvian flare-up beneath it, however, the interior may or may not wax warm.

Perhaps to more clearly distinguish the two, barbecuing in the original sense of the craft came to be called, by many of its devotees, smoke cooking. Here the fare to be prepared, often a tougher cut of meat such as brisket or pork shoulder, is allowed to cook slowly and indirectly in the smoke of the fire rather than in the flames. The temperature is usually kept within 20 degrees F. of the boiling point of water, on one side or the other, and it's kept there almost forever or until the meat is so tender that it's ready to fall apart, whichever comes first.

If timing is everything, then everything can take its time in smoke cooking, as I discovered during my initiation to the ceremony that night so many years ago. It wasn't nighttime when we started the ritual. It was more like three in the afternoon, with dinner planned for a leisurely seven o'clock. My initiator, Patrick Crow, a New York editor from Arkansas who had developed a culinary leaning toward pesto and other refinements laminated onto his hometown good-old-boy penchant for the simpler things in life, fished some marinating pork chops from a bowl on the kitchen counter of his summer place upstate, piled them onto a plate, grabbed a bottle of homemade barbecue sauce, and took me out back.

I'd expected to find there a traditional grill. Instead I found this black missile nose cone on three legs. It was labeled "Brinkmann."

"A silo smoker," Pat explained, removing the tip of the nose cone.

The coals were already glowing nicely in the missile, so I was rather surprised when he pulled some soggy pieces of wood from a bucket of water nearby and proceeded to kill the fire by putting them on top of the coals. "That's for more smoke," he informed me. Well, he certainly got what he asked for.

Next he set a pan of water above the hissing wood. Finally, the chops went on the grill and the cover back on the smoker. The bottle of sauce and the empty plate went on a rock beside the billowing contraption.

"Let's go for a walk," Pat said.

My eyebrows must have shot up, for he added, "The water will keep the meat moist. We'll come back in a couple of hours and swab it down with some more sauce." And so we abandoned the contraption, massive curtains of smoke curling around its lid, and headed up into the hills.

A couple of hours later, the sky turned black. The wind ripped leaves off the trees, and it was raining sideways. We discovered all the hills weren't exactly where we'd left them going out. Our return was delayed until eight o'clock.

Pat strode confidently to the smoker, lifted the lid, and speared the chops. Plate in hand and dripping wet, he entered the house. I was in time to see twin dubious looks — one directed toward him by his wife, Elizabeth, one toward me by mine, Susan. "Done to perfection," Pat reported cheerfully.

We sat down to some of the best chops I'd ever tasted. The following day, I went out and purchased a smoker.

As so often happens with the best-laid plans, the exigent problems of day-to-day life, more work than civilized life should allow, and an unusually severe early cold snap that turned the tomatoes in the garden into Popsicles conspired to keep the smoker in its carton for most of that fall. Then Thanksgiving rolled around — and talk of turkey.

Now turkey, save for its place in tradition, was never a favorite dish of mine. I would put on my plate a dutiful slice of the dark meat, a little more flavorsome and moist than the white, and fill the remainder of the space with copious quantities of Susan's chestnut stuffing, considerably more to my liking.

"Why not smoke the turkey?" was the inspired suggestion.

"The whole thing?" I expostulated. "We're talking twenty-five pounds here! With the stuffing, that could take several days."

"Well, I could cook the dressing separately in the oven," Susan offered.

Thus it was that we smoked our first turkey. It took some nine hours to cook, and when we finally pulled the bird from the smoker, it had the appearance of a boulder-size piece of anthracite.

What do you do at seven o'clock on a Thanksgiving evening with some twenty guests awaiting dinner and an anthracitic turkey?

Well, I reasoned at last, we always ate by candlelight on this occasion, and if we moved the candles far away, perhaps, with all the fixings, no one would notice the diminished aspect of the bird. Carving in the flickering dark, I served and sliced and served and sliced until we'd whittled that bird down to the bare bones. None of us had ever had such turkey — succulent, flavorsome, a little smoky, supremely tender.

Our Thanksgiving crowd, a disparate group of friends met over the years in a host of different places, arrive from various states and even countries — England is usually represented, France on occasion, others randomly — and hence generally stay for several days. Dinner on the Friday after Thanksgiving soon evolved into an informal lamb barbecue.

For many years, we had our own flock of sheep and an ample supply of joints to roast. We did it colonial-style, on an old-fashioned revolving iron grate on the hearth before the blazing fire. We would sit and watch the flames, rotating the grate occasionally, while we talked in the quiet dusk of the late November evening.

The year following the occasion of our first smoked turkey, the Thanksgiving gathering somehow, through various invitations and welcome but unexpected drop-ins, reached forty-five guests by the Wednesday noon of the big holiday. We added a fish and a venison course to the Thursday feast. For the Friday barbecue, however, clearly a couple of joints on the hearth would not suffice. To serve that number, a whole roast lamb would be more in order.

So it was that I proposed something that would put me irrevocably into the camp of true-blue smoke chefs — namely, a proper barbecue pit.

"Where?" asked Susan.

"Why, there, of course." I pointed to the open sunny lawn outside the bay window of the dining nook. "It's convenient to the kitchen, easy to clean up, and," I expounded on my chosen theme, "all that alkaline ash will help balance our acid New England soil."

I've never quite determined whether Susan really falls for my impromptu rationalizations or merely humors them, but, whichever is the case, the lunch crowd was eager to pitch in. Come dinnertime, the lawn featured a pit some five feet long, three feet wide, and two feet deep. A couple of the menfolk, with an enthusiastic youngster in tow, had taken the tractor and trailer into the woods and returned with half a cord of air-dried hickory from a tree the beavers had thoughtfully felled that spring and left hung up on an adjacent maple.

On the morning of the Friday lamb roast, the sky began clouding over while we were pounding forked goalposts into the earth at either end of the open-air hearth to support the roasting spit. By the time we had a blaze started in the pit, the temperature had begun to drop noticeably. As the lamb, nicely studded with garlic cloves and rosemary, was hoisted above the coals on a six-foot pry bar pressed into service as a rotisserie spit, the outdoor thermometer was registering in the mid-thirties. Shortly thereafter, it began to snow.

One of the things that makes New England memorable, they say, is its four distinct seasons — which you sometimes get all in one day. The roasting of an entire lamb was not a mission that could be removed in inclement weather to the comfort of the kitchen, nor could we repair to the living room with the laden spit. Our fireplace was not the walk-in variety. There was nothing for it but to persist.

To shield the fire from the wind, now gusting to twenty-five miles per hour, we brought over a couple of sheets of spare plywood from the barn. To support the plywood, we brought over some vertical nesting boxes from an old chicken coop we were dismantling to convert into horse stalls. To keep the snow from snuffing out the fire, for by now we had several inches of the white stuff, we draped a large blue tarp over the pit.

Robert Abel, an old friend and long-standing Thanksgiving guest, took over supervision of the hand-turned spit. The rest of us supplied alternate samples of dry and wet wood to keep the fire smoldering and served our stint rotating the pry bar. The procedure was to face the fire until icicles formed on one's back, then turn one's back to the fire until icicles formed in front.

Some eight hours into this operation of smoking the lamb and ourselves, I was in the kitchen mixing up a fresh pitcher of hot buttered rum for the team when Janet, another longtime Thanksgiving guest, pointed out the window at our glowing structure. "Amazing."

My heart swelled at this appreciation of our resourcefulness.

"How did you do that?" she mused wonderingly. "You guys took paradise and in a matter of hours converted it into a slum."

Well, no matter. The lamb was great, and we've smoked one every Thanksgiving Friday since, although the ancillary structure has long since been replaced by a more permanent and attractive arrangement — a stone fire pit adjoining the terrace — and, no longer shepherds ourselves, we rely on a friend to supply the meat. The ash, by the way, didn't improve our lawn noticeably when I finally got around to filling in the pit.

On the subject of alkalinity and such, smoke cooking has a lot to offer those on a low-sodium diet, for salt plays a surprisingly small role in this means of food preparation. The more assertive spices and the smoke seasoning used somehow make salt largely unnecessary unless one is smoke-curing portions of meat, a preservative technique quite different from smoking used as a means of cookery.

By the same token, either salted or unsalted butter can be used in most of the recipes presented in this book. You'll find unsalted specified only where it's expressly needed, as the butter in many people's larder is at least lightly salted.

In giving the ingredients for a given recipe, I have listed the basic staple form easily procured in supermarkets, with rare exceptions such as cardamom, ever so much more flavorsome when its aromatic seeds are first removed from their white pods, and a few foreign spices available in specialty markets. By all means use fresh seasonings, however, if you have a ready source of them, and grind the spices yourself if you will, as I often do myself.

Experimentation is part of the fun of barbecuing. So don't hesitate to try a new and different spice here and there. Barbecue sauces in particular lend themselves to almost infinite variation. Hence a chapter of the book is devoted specifically to exploring some of their diversity, and in the sources listed at the back of the book, you'll find more avenues to scout for ideas. Just don't let your search distract you from that priceless interlude reserved for relaxing by the smoker— at leisure, content, surrounded by pleasant scents and sounds and conversation—which is what so much of smoke cooking is all about.

2. MASTERING THE SMOKE

B eer and Coke are the traditional beverages of choice for a smoky barbecue. Some say that's because of this cooking method's proletarian ancestry. Others claim it's because greasy fingerprints don't show up on cans and bottles the way they do on, say, fine wineglasses. Still others maintain that the association came about because rich, full-bodied fare overpowers more delicately flavored beverages. By my own reckoning, it's because beer or Coke and smoked foods just happen to be a great taste combination. Often, in fact, beer and, yes, Coke are even used as marinades, not to mention bastes, in smoke cooking.

Nonetheless, it's not that universal American symbol, the Coke, that makes smoke cooking a particular legacy of these shores. Rather it's our pioneer heritage. In the vast expanses of our once seemingly limitless country, torching a whole tree to roast one pig was not considered an extravagance. It was simply a practicality. The pig was tough from running around all that bountiful countryside, and there were a lot more important things to be done than monitoring a fire for maximum fuel efficiency — things such as sitting down with a good jug of corn mash after a hard day's work.

This, of course, was in a time before the advent of the cell phone and the portable fax, a time when people paced their lives to the seasons rather than the call of a beeper. Yet for all the hustle and bustle of these present days, the idea of stopping to smell the flowers is beginning to return to our thinking. And the aroma of smoke from a long, lazy cooking fire should be right up there with the lilacs.

For most of us, though, there's no going back to the primitive fire pit. In an efficiency- and gadgetry-oriented consumer society, the right smoke requires the right equipment.

This is not to put down gadgetry. Certain contrivances — some amazingly simple ones, in fact, like the chimney charcoal starters available today for firing up a smoker — make life far easier and more pleasant. That, to me, is the hallmark of a useful device.

When it comes to appropriate smoke technology, the basics are fairly simple. You need a place for the fire, a water pan, room for the food, and a way to cover them all so that the heat and the smoke and the moisture surround whatever's being cooked.

Probably the first outfit to put all this together was Brinkmann, granddaddy of the water smokers, as they've become known. These smokers look pretty much alike, taking the generic form of a miniature silo roosting on squat legs and topped by a handled dome. The silo itself is usually a single column nowadays. Then again, it may consist of two nested segments, as the original Brinkmann did, providing easier access to the interior. Either way, inside the silo are one or two grates to hold the food, a water pan, and, at the bottom, a heat source.

Charcoal is the most traditional fuel used by these smokers, but gas and electric models also are available, the smoky flavor in their case deriving from wood chips added to the main heat source. My own sentiment is that if it isn't sooty, it isn't a real smoker, but there are those who cite the convenience, as they see it, of a gas or an electric cooker.

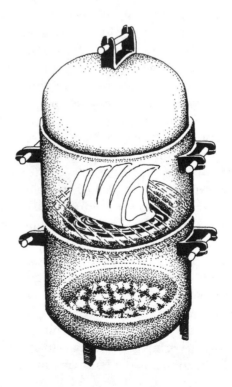

Sure, it's easier to maintain a constant temperature in a gas cooker — provided you remembered to shut off the gas valve after your last barbecue. If you didn't, you'll have to drive out to get the canister refilled. The electric smoker will keep an even temperature, too — provided you have an extension cord long enough and can find it. Then again, would you rather check the wood supply in the smoker every now and then while you're topping off drinks on the terrace or watch the electricity meter spin? Certainly smoke cooking is designed to be easy, but a bit of puttering lends the occasion an aura of accomplishment and satisfaction. Otherwise one might as well call for a pizza delivery.

Among the charcoal cookers, if you can find an old two-section silo smoker like the one Brinkmann used to make, do snap it up. In my opinion, this early design is superior to the modern one-piece construction featuring a fueling door on the side.

When the version with the door first came out, I bought one immediately, thinking it was a great idea. No more lifting off the top silo section with its grill and food and finding a safe place to put it down. No more hoisting the water pan out of the way to add coals to the fire pan.

Well, it was a great idea that didn't really work. Shaking live coals in through the little door can be an awkward affair, for the water pan is in the way. Replenishing the water supply can also be awkward, although I've remedied that problem somewhat with the aid of a long-spouted Haws watering can.

All the same, for most tending tasks I end up lifting the cover off the smoker anyhow, and now, since there's no middle section, I have to reach way down inside the silo to fish out the water pan before I can get at the fire pan. I'm hoping Brinkmann will bring back its classic original model one of these days.

Another basic type of cooker besides the silo is the kettle grill, developed by Weber. When Weber first came out with a covered grill, it was as much an innovation as the chimney erected in old British manors to replace the smoke hole in the roof. The Weber was originally designed for straight high-heat grilling. The covered kettle with its adjustable vents, conceived to maximize heat convection for sizzling backyard steaks and burgers, allowed one to control the cooking temperature far better than an ordinary, open grill did.

What Weber didn't realize at the time was that this device was also ideal for smoke cooking. Covered kettle cookers can easily be adapted for smoking provided a water pan is placed inside in such

a manner that the food being cooked is exposed only to indirect heat and the top and bottom draft vents are shut almost all the way, effectively reducing the fire's intensity.

The water container for a kettle smoker can be of any kind so long as it's heatproof and fits inside the cooker without crowding the coals or cutting off the heat convection too much. Most kettle grills, since they were initially designed for what's essentially outdoor broiling, do not come with their own water pan. I use an aluminum roasting pan to good advantage here.

The pan can either be set in the middle of the coals and flanked with them or placed to one side on the coal grate, directly below the hood vent, in which case the coals should be pushed to the other side, over the bottom vent. I prefer the centered pan arrangement because the water stays hotter and better disperses its moisture from that position between the coals. The food to be smoked is placed on the grill directly above the water pan, never above the coals. This ensures that the food is cooked only with indirect heat and smoke. Also, any drippings end up in the water pan rather than the fire, where they could cause flare-ups.

Gas grills such as the Ducane, Sterling, and similar covered cookers featuring both a lower and an upper rack can be used for smoking provided there is room for a water pan between the gas burners and the food rack and provided a tray for wood chips can be added close enough to the heat source for the chips to smolder. The rotisserie models are particularly adaptable to smoking in that by design they usually provide room directly beneath the spit for a drip tray, so a water pan can be placed there and chips arranged around it. Because of the heat intensity likely to build up inside the gas grills, however, you may have to prop the lid open partway at times in order to keep the temperature low enough for smoke cooking.

Some box-type gas smokers overcome the problem of overheating by putting out less heat than a standard gas grill does in the first place. The Jurgens smoker, for instance, has a heat output of only 10,000 Btu, about one-third that of a regular gas grill. In addition, its core of pipes is laid out in such a way as to distribute the heat over an area larger than that warmed by the flames alone. It also has a deflector to keep the flames covered. All these features help to ensure the slow cooking that true barbecuing requires. A water tray and two chip trays provide the means for supplying the necessary moisture and smoke. I find the water tray skimpy, and although wood chips placed above the burner do supply excellent smoke, the trays need frequent replenishing.

An innovative option is incorporated into the Rotisserie Master

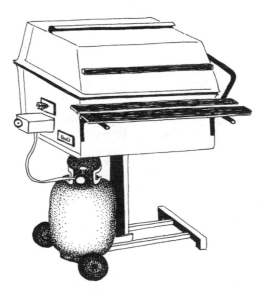

from Swisher. Outfitted with a roasting spit, the charcoal-fired Swisher seems a rather ordinary smoker rotisserie, and I find the spit clumsy to work with because it doesn't lift out as a unit. To load it up, you have to hold it by its attached motor; push it through a small hole in the supporting wall on one side of the grill; put the first set of anchoring prongs on it; spear the chicken or the joint or whatever you're smoking and balance it properly; secure it with the second pair of prongs; and finally, after all that, somehow manage to thread the rod through the second little hole on the other side of the grill — all while hanging on to the meat inside the hot smoker.

This somewhat awkward design notwithstanding, the spit is utterly transformed by the ingenious set of grilling trays supplied with it. They ride on the spit as if it were a Ferris wheel, and each of the four shelves can be loaded with different fare — burgers, chicken wings, fish, veggies, anything you can think of. People seem to love reaching in and collaring choice morsels from the swinging trays as they roll by.

Another unusual attachment available for the Swisher is a solar panel to power the rotisserie motor. At first I thought this item a bit of an absurdity, and I purchased it only because our son, Revell, a solar power maven, thought it was so cool. However, it turned out to be a most useful device. We do a lot of our summer barbecuing down by the pond, far from any source of electricity, and the spit just keeps on cranking, even on cloudy days.

Many early homemade barbecue "pits" were simply barrels cut in half lengthwise. Such a barrel smoker was set on its side, the two halves joined with hinges, and outfitted with a grill in the middle.

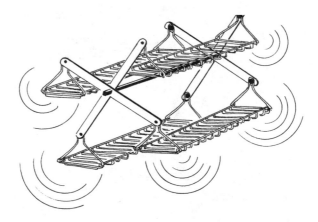

The bottom half held the wood supply; the top lifted for access to the grill. Today there's a whole range of barrel, or drum, smokers, their myriad suppliers including Oklahoma Joe's, Klose, Hondo, Pioneer, and Lang.

These modern barrel smokers feature a separate, offset firebox, located at one end of the cooking chamber, for better heat control. Some of these drum cookers now even have a third chamber attached to the barrel, opposite the firebox, to supply cool smoke for the ardent aficionado of smoke curing, the long, slow variant of smoking used as a means of preservation. These improved barrel smokers range from standard backyard-barbecue-size models offered at standard backyard-barbecue prices to trailer-mounted cookers with price tags just this side of the cost of a compact car.

In the category of the unusual, the most extraordinary smoker I've ever cooked in is probably the Kamado. Introduced from Japan, the Kamado is not, as one might first suspect, the latest high-tech electronic wonder from that ultragadgetized country. Rather it's a covered ceramic tub whose design claims a vintage of several thousand years. Cooking with such a vessel was the standard way of preparing a hot meal in Japan prior to the introduction of modern gas and electric stoves. The very name *Kamado* is an untranslatable Japanese word that I've been told conveys the essence of cooker, smoker, stove, and fireplace all in one.

The Kamado is singularly heavy. The wheeled dolly available for it is a necessity if you plan to move it at all, and even so mounted, it can be rolled only over a smooth surface such as a concrete terrace or a wooden deck with the smallest of cracks between the planks.

This smoker also can't be left out in the rain, but must be covered in inclement weather, because it tends to absorb water and then crack when fired up. And yes, I admit to not always properly protecting my smokers from the elements. Truth to tell, the family some time ago dubbed my original Brinkmann "Trusty Rusty." Privately, I think of it affectionately as my rustic smoker.

Possessing a degree of fragility because of its ceramic construction, something not encountered in the other smokers, the Kamado is nevertheless one of the most versatile and economical charcoal cookers on the market. With no exaggeration, it can claim a range of operating temperatures extending from a low of 150 degrees F. to a high of 700 degrees F. It can also legitimately boast of exceptional fuel efficiency, attributable to its thick ceramic walls that retain heat so effectively. In fact, the biggest difficulty you'll encounter cooking with a Kamado may well be adjusting to the lower fuel consumption and not letting the internal temperature soar too high.

The smoker doesn't come with a thermometer of its own, and in view of the cooker's versatile temperature range, I highly recommend installing one. I used a three-eighth-inch masonry drill to bore a hole in the lid of mine large enough to accommodate the sensor of a Taylor #5972 candy thermometer, which will record any temperature falling between 100 and 400 degrees F.

A thermometer is a most helpful addition to any smoker, for that matter. The built-in meters found on some cookers, indicating sweeping ranges marked "cold," "warm," and "hot," aren't of much use to the chef trying to keep the temperature of the smoker at a steady 210 to 230 degrees F., say. You want something more accurate than that.

A meat thermometer will test for doneness in a particular cut and is handy for worrisome categories like pork. Usually, though, the highest temperature a meat thermometer will register is 200 degrees F., so it's not much help in gauging the heat inside a smoker. An ordinary oven thermometer will certainly give you an accurate reading of that, but you won't be able to see it without lifting the lid off the smoker, letting valuable heat escape every time you do so.

No, for gauging the internal temperature of a smoker, what you really need is that candy thermometer. It's quite as possible — much easier, in fact — to drill through the lid of most steel smokers as it is to drill through the ceramic Kamado. When the probe of the candy thermometer is inserted in the three-eighth-inch aperture you've bored, the face is conveniently readable above the smoker's dome. I've equipped any number of my cookers with heat indicators by this means. In the case of a vented model like the Weber, the accessorizing is even simpler. The probe can easily be slipped through the top draft vent of the cooker.

Once you've worked with a particular cooker for a while, you'll probably be able to assess the degree of heat inside by simply listening to your smoker. Although the various cookers on the market all have their individual idiosyncrasies, when you've become accustomed to yours, you'll be able to take its temperature by the sound of the water simmering in its pan — or not simmering, as the case may be. The purr of liquid bubbling will be heard as the water reaches its boiling point of 212 degrees F., an almost ideal temperature for much of smoke cooking.

It should be noted, however, that where the cooking time is very long and the meat or fowl very high in fat content, eventually enough of the fat will melt and drip down into the water pan to form a film over the water. This is all to the good. The fat of the fare is reduced and the flavor intensified. On the other hand, the savory film spread over the water will also dampen that purr of bubbles — until the temperature rises much higher and the liquid roils with heat. The candy thermometer does make life easier.

Another thermometer handy to have around, although not wholly necessary, is a quick-registering meat thermometer for the fare itself. Because smoke cooking is done at low temperatures, it's always possible for a particular dish to have all the outward appearance of being cooked to perfection and yet be scarcely warm inside. Checking the internal temperature, particularly of a pork dish, is a good idea.

A given temperature inside a smoker — or inside whatever's on the grill, for that matter — presupposes that you got a fire started in the first place. Now for the chef presiding over a gas or an electric cooker, this is not a problem, barring an empty gas canister or a misplaced extension cord, respectively. The obligatory feat is accomplished by opening a valve or throwing a switch. For the dyed-in-the-wool charcoal barbecuer like myself, on the other hand, the issue is not so simple. Those stolid briquettes must be cajoled into really burning, not just going a little gray around the edges and quietly expiring.

Flammable liquid starters, gasoline, and other smoke foulers are no-no's. So are impregnated briquettes. Both can make food taste like the motor wipe rag at your local garage.

The time-honored method of starting a fire in the smoker is interchangeable with the one for starting a campfire, except that in the wilderness one doesn't have the benefits of the day's newspaper and charcoal briquettes. In the version for the smoker, one crumples up the paper, adds twigs, then larger sticks, then a mound of charcoal. With luck, the paper lights the twigs, the twigs ignite the larger sticks, and eventually the charcoal pile is all aglow. With lack of luck, one huffs and one puffs, or one fans away.

Our son, Revell, one day improved upon these supportive measures. Noting my reddening face as I labored to convey oxygen to a lifeless fire pan, this enterprising fifteen-year-old ran to the garage and retrieved a junked leaf blower given to him by someone for parts but still functional, along with the extension cord from the workbench. And so it was that I learned how a leaf blower can better the best of bellows.

Eventually, a more dedicated device replaced the leaf blower. I chanced upon a product called a Charcoal Chimney, a number of whose clones have now become widely available. I heartily recommend one of these devices, a rarity among gadgets in that it actually does what it claims to do — namely, effortlessly ignite charcoal briquettes.

Basically, a Charcoal Chimney is simply a handled, dual-compartment cylinder made of sheet steel, its bottom chamber perforated. Put the briquettes in the top half of the cylinder, crumple a sheet of newspaper, wad the bottom with it, set the chimney on your grill or in any other safe spot nearby, and light the paper. I find that once the first sheet has burned to ashes, it pays to crumple up and light a second one. In any case, that's all there is to starting a fire with a Charcoal Chimney. The cylinder just sits there smoking a bit, and 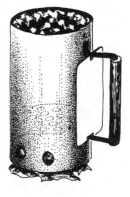 in 15 to 20 minutes, through the magic of convection, all the coals are glowing. Dump them into the smoker pan, and you have fire.

Speaking of pans, owners of gas and electric grills are apt to find the Gas Grill Smoker, available through the Grill Lover's Catalog, among others, a well-nigh indispensable accessory once they've tried it. You put wood chips into this box, close the slotted cover, and place the box on the fire grate directly above the flames or, in the case of an electric grill, on the char diamond of the heating element. Soon flavorful smoke is emanating from the smoldering chips without their making a mess of your grill.

Another mess preventer is the Grill Topper, available by that name or in the form of similar replicas for most grill configurations, including the round ones of the silo and kettle smokers. Made of porcelain-clad steel, these small-holed add-on grills not only keep delicate foods in their place but are dishwasher safe as well.

Lest I create the impression that I'm a supertidy person, let me hasten to say that I'm not. However, nothing brings me back to the humdrum side of reality after a relaxing barbecue quite as effectively as does trying to clean up a gooey grill. As for doing it the next day, when everything has congealed, well, that's even worse.

The particular mess that the Grill Topper averts is the one left by succulently basted shrimp and other small, soft foods slipping through the bars of the grate to the water pan. Here, I suppose, what I resent is not so much the mess they make as the fact that the fire got what I didn't.

For taking things on and off the grill, by the way, frankly, I prefer a sturdy, old-fashioned three-pronged kitchen fork to the tongs ordained on the barbecue circuit. You will be told over and over again by smoking aficionados that you should use tongs so as not to pierce the meat and let the juices out. I suppose it must have been Archimedes who said, "Give me tongs large enough, and I will lift an ox." Whatever the case, I personally find lifting anything but shrimp, sausages, and chicken breasts with tongs a most awkward maneuver.

Speaking of awkward maneuvers, juggling hot grills, water pans, and smoker lids can be difficult, if not impossible, without a good set of long-armed insulated mitts to keep from being burned. Don't try to get away with just one. You really need a pair.

Most of the other utensils you might need for smoke cooking you'll probably find by raiding the kitchen drawers. The exception that comes to mind is the mop. For good down-home mopping of the meat, most barbecuers use one of those small all-cotton dishwashing mops. Messy they may be, but they can really slather on the sauce, and when basting, you don't want to be stingy. Sure, you can dab a bit of sauce onto the meat with a brush, being careful not to get a drop on the grill. But neatness isn't what smoking is all about.

Mops, brushes, tongs, forks — they're all a matter of personal choice. After a few barbecues, you'll know which implements work best for you. You'll also know for certain that a particular fork or spatula produced the magic touch that produced the perfect dish that made an evening perfect. And then you'll be able to relax and enjoy smoke cooking to the hilt, because you'll also know that you've mastered real barbecuing.

3. THE RIGHT SMOKE

L ow heat, a long time, and lots of smoke — those are the keys to a good barbecue, whatever particular smoker and accessories you use. Now the smoke from different woods has long been claimed to enhance the taste of particular victuals, and each association of fuel and fare has its devotees. For instance, alder was traditionally used by the Indians of the Northwest for smoking salmon, and barbecue aficionados will tell you that alder imparts a light, delicate flavor that doesn't overpower the relatively mild taste of the salmon. It's a politically correct choice of heat as well.

Nevertheless, the original reason for using alder was probably that it's a fast-growing, easy-to-cut wood that happens to grow copiously along the waters where the salmon run. Considering that the only other trees common to the same terrain are pine and spruce, both of which impart a resinous, bitter tang to foods smoked over them, the initial choice of fuel here was most likely dictated less by refined sensibilities than by simple expediency.

Different woods do make a difference, and there really are people who can distinguish ribs smoked over an alder fire from those redolent of hickory. There are also people who can differentiate between a 1983 chardonnay pressed from grapes grown on the southern slope of a vineyard and the 1986 vintage harvested from the western side of the same vineyard. However, there's no more reason to be intimidated by expert opinions on the proper wood to use for a particular dish than there is to be cowed by connoisseurs of vintages. For most of us, what counts about either a wine or a meal is that it tastes good, and for successful barbecuing the fuel need only supply low heat and a pleasant smoke from honest wood.

Most home smoke cooking is done with charcoal briquettes as the main heat source. There are important differences in the various briquettes on the market, though. Looking like nothing so much as identical lumps of coal designed by Raymond Lowe, they nonetheless vary considerably in both burning duration and heat efficiency.

Briquettes are essentially the charred remains of incinerated sawdust bound together with regular coal dust, various starches, and a whole bunch of strange substances, including some flammable ones. By the time the sawdust is turned into carbon, most of the wood flavor has burned away. The mixed-in additives, on the other hand, often retain their flavor and can contribute in an unwanted fashion to the taste of your food. So don't just pick up any old briquettes for your smoker. While you may have to do some sampling and shopping around for them, find a brand that provides consistent heat output without a consistent chemical aftertaste, and then stick with it.

In Connecticut, where we live, there still exist a number of real charcoal manufacturers. The lump hardwood charcoal they make is bagged and sold just like briquettes, but there's a big difference between the two products. In the lump charcoal, you can actually see the cells and even the tree rings of the carbonized wood, and the chunks range from pea-size bits to slabs six to eight inches long.

For the ultimate smoke, specialty charcoals are procurable by mail. For instance, true-blue enthusiasts can now order bags of the same charcoal once used in distilling the famous Jack Daniel's Tennessee sipping whiskey.

Real hardwood charcoal, though more expensive than briquettes, burns much longer and hotter than briquettes do, so a smaller amount is needed per fire. Because of its efficiency, when you use it for the first time, start out with less rather than more, and keep a careful eye on the temperature inside your smoker. Switching from briquettes to real charcoal is like going from a Volkswagen to a Ferrari. It takes some getting used to.

A third fuel choice is plain dried hardwood. A little planning is in order if you go this route. You'll need to gather the wood, and for that you'll need a tree. However, if there happen to be a couple of mature maples or other hardwoods in your yard, your annual cleanup of fallen twigs and branches will probably yield enough wood for several good barbecues.

Together with your main fuel source, you're going to need some smoking wood, as it's called, as well. Briquettes have no real flavoring value, or if they do, it's liable to be none that you want. Hardwood charcoal has a certain satisfying air about it when it's burning, but not enough to supply that ethereal smoky aura so indispensable to smoke cookery. For that you need some fragrant wet wood — you want this wood to smolder, not burn. For a gas or an electric smoker, you'll need wood chips.

In choosing your smoking wood, about the only thing you have to worry about is staying away from any tree bearing needles — pine, spruce, and such — unless you like the taste of resin. Even this rule is not ironclad, though. For instance, I've found that juniper yields a flavorsome, if robust, smoke that's very appealing as a change from, say, the sweeter aroma of the fruitwoods.

Mesquite is au courant these days, largely, I suspect, because of its mystique and the popularity of Tex-Mex cooking. Yet the traditional hardwoods—oak, hickory, maple, and fruitwoods such as apple — are just as good, if not better, for smoke cooking. Then again, mesquite is a southwestern wood, so that may simply be my northerner's mentality showing.

In our area, maple is often the wood of choice for smoke among barbecue chefs, in part simply because it's so readily available. Maple, traditionally associated with ham, lends most other fare an agreeable mild taste as well.

Hickory and its southern cousin, the pecan, have the same porcine association. Stronger than maple in flavor, they are commonly found smoldering beneath more highly sauced dishes like ribs and, in the beef category, brisket.

Oak has a perceptible acid note — what in wine circles is known as an assertive taste. An excellent choice for beef dishes, it's also fine for just about anything else save perhaps fish.

Fruitwoods such as apple and pear — but not cherry, which tends to produce an acrid smoke — are good choices that will infuse any food with a sparkling flavor. Again, these woods are associated with ham, but that's partly because this particular joint is one of the most commonly smoked meats. Fruitwoods also work surprisingly well with vegetables.

Alder is another fine choice of smoke wood. We have no shortage of freshly cut alder at our place during the summer barbecue season. In fact, we have rather too much of this commodity, strewn along the banks of our pond and river courtesy of a local beaver colony. I go down and harvest it as needed, muttering darkly under my breath about the possibilities of a career in orthodontics specializing in wiring castor jaws shut.

Not that beavers limit themselves to alder, for they don't. A spot on the north side of the pond used to be called Twin Oak Point.

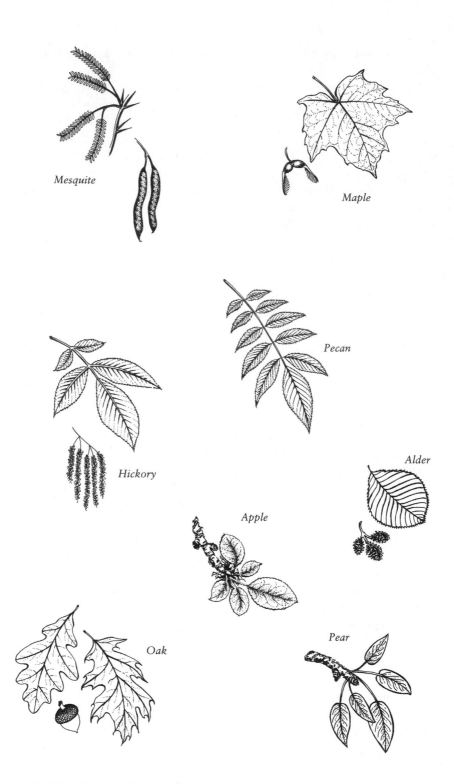

Mesquite

Maple

Pecan

Hickory

Alder

Apple

Pear

Oak

Grapevine

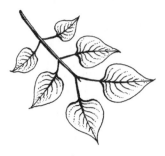
Lilac

Then a few years ago, it became Lone Oak Point. Last year it was rechristened No Oak Point. As I said, in the country, finding smoke wood is not a problem.

In choosing your wood for smoke, don't neglect the trimmings from your garden. In France, the wood from grapevines is much prized for the savor it imparts to cooked foods. In New England, where lilac is common, this bush's purple heartwood is treasured for its uncommonly fragrant smoke.

For use in the efficient, backyard-size smokers of today, the wood you choose for smoke needs to be in chunks small enough to become saturated when immersed in water, so they won't dry out too quickly in the fire pan and generate too much heat. To supply copious smoke, the pieces need to be really waterlogged.

Normally, I cut branches one inch or more in diameter into disks one to two inches thick. Smaller branches I break into four-inch lengths. I sink them all in a bucket of water to soak overnight or longer. I'm inclined to keep a bucketful of wet wood handy in case the urge to smoke up a dish overtakes me suddenly. If you acquire this same preparative habit, do also cultivate the practice of changing the water every couple of days. Otherwise you're apt to have a bucket of very slimy wood on your hands.

Besides your wood chunks, another excellent source of smoke, and one that will have everyone around the cooker oohing and aahing over its fragrance, is herb wood. Here rosemary and sage come to mind.

Our family first encountered sage-smoked fare when we were living in a tiny village by the name of Restinclières in southern France. Exploring the nearby mountain byways, we would often pass a small, neat sign reading FERME posted by some winding drive appearing to go nowhere. I dimly recalled, from a meager mastery of

Rosemary

Sage

French well rusted by the passage of years, that *ferme* was the French word for "closed," and I kept wondering why there were CLOSED signs marking driveways one probably wouldn't want to randomly drive up anyhow. NO TRESPASSING I could understand, but CLOSED? This implied that at some point in time, they must be open. Why?

Finally, out of sheer curiosity, we somewhat timorously drove down one of these "closed" lanes. At its end, we came upon a small farm in whose yard, together with a placid herd of goats, were half a dozen parked cars. We got out of ours to inquire and found that we had happened on a charming, tiny, intimate country restaurant. There we dined on delectable lamb cooked over an open fire whose coals were laced with smoldering sprigs of sage.

It was only as we were leaving that, looking more closely at the sign when we turned onto the main roadway again, I realized that there was no accent on the second *e*, which, come to think of it, the *fermé* I remembered used to have. A quick look in the dictionary we faithfully carried with us showed that, sure enough, those myriad driveways we'd passed with little signs beside them weren't closed at all, but rather welcomed visitors to "farms" serving enchanting rural repasts.

One of the pleasures we brought back with us from Restinclières was the custom of adding a few green — as in greenwood — sprigs of sage to the coals when smoking lamb dishes. In fact, planting a little sage near the spot where the smoker usually sits isn't a bad idea at all. The bush's foliage is an attractive gray-green, and the trimmings are an olfactory delight. Rosemary is another garden addition to consider tucking in near the smoker, where sprays of the fragrant leaves can be harvested at a moment's notice to add their distinctive savor to fuel or fare, notably lamb and fish.

With a supply of basic fuel on hand and the smoke wood for your barbecue soaking in its bucket, you have only a few small details left to tend to before settling down for a leisurely afternoon of company by the smoker while the cooking tends to itself. There's the matter of the water pan, for instance.

Unless you're using a disposable aluminum pan of the kind suggested for a Weber or similar cooker, line the water pan of your smoker with heavy-duty aluminum foil to keep it from becoming crusted with burned drippings from the meat, difficult at best to clean up. Besides, there will be times when you want to save the drippings for gravy stock.

Another consideration is the water itself. Start out with hot water, and you'll have much more constant heat in your smoker. A lot of energy goes into heating cold water, and when a smoker's busy doing that, all of a sudden it's not as hot as it used to be, so you add more coals. Then the water warms up, the extra coals are all aglow, and now the smoker's too hot. It's easier to start with preheated water.

If the temperature does rise too high in your smoker, by the way, that's easy enough to remedy. Simply prop the cover open a bit. I use any old stick I find lying around, but there are high-tech hood holders, complete with heat-dissipating handles, that will do the job more elegantly.

Another way to regulate the heat inside a charcoal smoker is to pile or spread out the briquettes, whichever is needed. Coals piled pyramid fashion provide more heat than a flat layer does.

Don't forget that real charcoal generates more heat per piece than briquettes do — and generates it more intensely, at that. Firewood provides the most heat of all, but it does necessitate more frequent feeding of the fire, because to keep the temperature from going through the roof, you have to use relatively little of it at a time, maintaining the long, slow smoke essential for a real barbecue.

Finally, speaking of long, slow smoking, don't underestimate the potential heat and fire hazard of yesterday's coals. I've often started a matchless fire in a barbecue a full twenty-four hours after the previous feast. Dispose of old coals very carefully, and make sure you locate your smoker where hot embers accidentally dropped will not start a smoldering fire. It's the dinner you want to undergo long, slow smoking, not the neighborhood.

4. RIBS, RIBS, AND MORE RIBS

R ibs are the essence of American barbecuing. Steak is great, hamburgers are always tasty, chicken is delicious, pork butt is superb, but extravagantly sauce-slathered, finger-licking-good, tender ribs — they're the real heart of a barbecue.

Barbecued ribs are all-American fare. Chinese restaurants serve them, both boneless and with handles, but those are a different species — spicy, yes, but delicate somehow. In Hungary, they make great stuffed veal ribs, but those are as closely related to barbecued ribs as stuffed paprikas are. Even in the lavish *churrascarias* of Brazil, down whose aisles are paraded all manner of grilled delicacies from chicken hearts to filet mignon to whole sword-skewered racks of steaks sliced individually with a flourish at your table, good gooey six-licks-and-three-napkins ribs are unheard-of.

As if to make up for this worldwide shortage of honest-to-goodness barbecued ribs, there are more versions of the dish in the United States than there are coals at a hog roast. Far be it from me to stick my neck out and pick the best. Here are a dozen rib recipes, all of which are well worth trying and all of which you'll probably sample over and over again without ever being able to determine your favorite.

In planning a rib barbecue, you can count on most smoke cookers to accommodate a 2½- to 3½-pound rack of ribs. If your smoker has a large grill like that of the big Weber or the oblong Jurgens, or if it will support a stacked pair of grills as the Brinkmann does, you can double the number of ribs to be smoked.

Another way to increase the rib capacity of your smoker is to use a rib rack, a wire frame available in several different conformations that allows you to stand the ribs on end. Rib racks work nicely for large numbers of ribs. They're particularly handy for cuts amply endowed with fat, permitting that element to drain freely and evenly from all sides into the water pan. Their only disadvantage is that a mop applied to vertical ribs, unless it's very, very thick, tends to drain away into the water pan as well.

If you do use a rib rack and the recipe you're following includes a baste, make sure you have a long-handled brush or mop with which to slather the stuff on the ribs during their long sojourn in the smoker. Otherwise you won't be able to work the liquid down between the individual ribs to keep them moist and succulent without smoking your fingers as well.

For two racks of ribs weighing out at 5 to 7 pounds, the same amount of rub as for one rack half that size will suffice, since all the rub you pat onto the ribs never sticks. However, you will need to double any mop recipe involved if you are to have enough sauce left, after basting both racks, to serve as a dip for the finished ribs. You can't set out too much sauce at a real barbecue.

SHAKE 'N' SMOKE RIBS

In the classic American barbecue, two separate steps — apart from the long, slow smoke, naturally — supply the distinctive flavor. First there's the rub, then there's the mop. Now this is different from seasoning meat by either a vinegary marinade or a dusting of spices before smoking. It's different, too, from simply basting the meat with barbecue sauce as it smokes.

A rub, sometimes referred to as a dry rub, draws a portion of the juices from a cut of meat to the surface, there to mingle with the seasoning and with it form a crust encasing the rest of the meat's juices and flavor.

The secret to concocting a good rub lies in not skimping on the ingredients. The mix must be ample enough to coat the meat completely, sealing it in spices.

One way to help achieve this objective is to dump both rub and ribs into a Ziploc-type plastic bag and shake the bag until the ribs are well covered with the seasoning. The bags designed for the freezer are a bit stronger than the regular storage ones, and I recommend this sturdier version for the aforesaid activity. Nothing spawns a sneeze storm quite as spectacularly as the sudden ripping of a gyrating bag full of peppery ribs.

SERVES 3 TO 4

2½- to 3½-pound rack of pork spareribs

THE RUB
⅔ cup firmly packed dark brown sugar
¼ cup paprika
2 tablespoons garlic powder
1 tablespoon ground cayenne pepper
1 tablespoon ground black pepper
1 tablespoon ground white pepper
2 teaspoons ground coriander
1 teaspoon salt

THE MOP

1 tablespoon butter
1 medium-size onion, finely chopped
8 cloves garlic, peeled and minced or put through a garlic press
1 twelve-ounce can tomato paste
1 cup red wine vinegar
½ cup water
½ cup molasses
½ cup firmly packed dark brown sugar
3 tablespoons Worcestershire sauce
3 tablespoons chili powder
1 tablespoon dry mustard

A day in advance of your planned barbecue, set the ribs out on a cutting board or a butcher block and slice between them one-third of the way in from both ends so that the rub can be worked in between the ribs.

For the rub, measure the brown sugar into a small mixing bowl and mash out any lumps with a fork. Add the paprika, garlic powder, and cayenne, black, and white peppers, followed by the coriander and salt. Blend these ingredients well and pour into a Ziploc-type plastic bag large enough to hold the ribs comfortably.

Add the ribs and shake the bag until they are thoroughly dusted with the rub. Refrigerate, tightly closed, overnight. Shake the bag once before going to bed and again in the morning.

About 5½ hours before you plan to serve the ribs, fire up your smoker and start putting the mop together.

For the mop, melt the butter in a medium-size stainless steel or flameproof ceramic saucepan set over low heat. Stir in the onion and garlic and sauté gently until golden. Add the tomato paste and mix well. Blend in the vinegar, water, and molasses. Add the brown sugar, Worcestershire sauce, and, a little at a time, the chili powder and dry mustard, stirring well after each addition. Simmer, stirring occasionally, for about 30 minutes, or until the sauce is thick. Remove from the heat and set aside until needed for basting.

Once the fire in your smoker has settled down to a good bed of coals that will last for a number of hours without too much tending, add a few chunks of wet wood or chips and put the ribs on the grill over a pan of hot water. Let smoke, covered and undisturbed, for about 2 hours.

At that point, open the smoker lid and baste the ribs well with the mop, taking this opportunity to check the coals in the fire pan and the liquid level in the water pan. Replenish as needed, adding wet wood for plenty of smoke as well. Cook the ribs for 3 hours more, turning and basting them after 1 hour and again after 2 hours. As always in smoke cooking, precise timing is not terribly important here. Just keep the smoke up and the temperature at 200 to 240 degrees F. and be liberal with your mopping.

By the end of their 5 hours on the grill, the ribs will have long since reached and passed the internal temperature of 160 to 170 degrees F. recommended for pork. But you can't overdo ribs by smoking, and the long, slow cooking will have rendered them tender to a tee.

About 10 minutes before you are ready to serve the ribs, treat them to a final mop, letting it set to a tantalizingly rich glaze over what may be the most succulent ribs you've ever tasted.

For finger-licking aficionados, provide yet more hot mop sauce served up in dipping bowls.

THE FOUR RIBS

SPARERIBS

Spareribs are cut from the elongated slab of bones located behind the pork shoulder. These are your archetypical barbecue ribs, America's favorite — long on flavor, long on bone, long-licking, but meager on the meat, hence the term *spare*.

LOIN OR BABY BACK RIBS

When it comes to meat, anything with the word *loin* in it equates to expensive, as in sirloin. These ribs are shorter than spareribs, hence the name *baby*, which refers not at all to the age of the pig involved. Baby back ribs are the yuppie contribution to barbecuing. Lean and tasty, they are meatier, less messy to eat, and, as you've already suspected, more costly than spareribs.

COUNTRY-STYLE RIBS

Country-style ribs, from immediately behind the upper portion of the pork shoulder known as the Boston butt, are part of the shoulder end of the loin. They are not true spareribs, any  more than baby back ribs are, being both meatier and fattier. However, while they contain more fat per pound of ribs, the fat is in the form of layers. The meat itself, between the layers, is leaner and less marbled than that of most ribs. Because of this, it's crucial to keep your water pan plentifully supplied when smoking country-style ribs, to prevent them from drying out. At the same time, these ribs benefit from parboiling, to reduce the fat layers, since fat doesn't drip away in smoking as much as it does in the hotter temperatures used for grilling. Country-style ribs are the meatiest of all ribs — and the messiest to eat.

SHORT RIBS

Now if baby back and country-style ribs aren't true spareribs, short ribs aren't even pork. They're trimmed from the plate end of the forequarter of beef known as the rib section, which supplies such highly prized steaks and roasts as the rib eye. They're not as tender as the rib cuts they adjoin, and they're also fattier, so parboiling is almost a necessity. However, when smoked, they 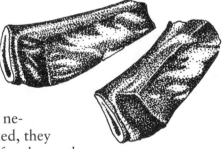 offer a flavorsome rib repast for those who don't eat pork — and some variety for those who do.

FIVE-SPICE RIBS

T he Chinese, probably the world's foremost consumers of pork, are very fond of barbecued spareribs. Dark mahogany-colored racks of them are displayed in butcher shop windows in every Chinatown I've ever visited, from San Francisco to London. They're a nibble that never fails to please.

The secret of these ribs' tastiness lies in the classic five-spice powder — a blend of star anise, cloves, cinnamon, fennel, and Szechuan peppercorns — used to flavor them. The fragrant mix quickly loses its pungency, so purchase it in small quantities or make a lot of these ribs — not a bad alternative.

SERVES 3 TO 4

2- to 3-pound rack of pork spareribs
1 teaspoon five-spice powder
1 teaspoon ground black pepper
½ teaspoon salt
3 tablespoons cooking sherry
3 tablespoons peanut oil
2 tablespoons honey
2 tablespoons hoisin sauce
1 tablespoon soy sauce
2 cloves garlic, peeled and put through a garlic press

The day before you plan to serve these ribs, lay the rack out on a large platter or dish and dust it on both sides with the five-spice powder, pepper, and salt. Let rest for at least 1 hour.

Meanwhile, measure into a small mixing bowl or pitcher the sherry, peanut oil, honey, hoisin sauce, soy sauce, and garlic. Stir well and pour this marinade over the spice-dusted ribs. Refrigerate, tightly covered, overnight.

Start your smoker heating 3½ to 4½ hours before dinnertime. When the coals are glowing, lift the rack of ribs from its marinade and place it on the grill. Reserve the marinade for basting.

Smoke the spareribs in the covered cooker for 3 to 4 hours at 200 to 240 degrees F. over good coals, some wet wood, and a pan of hot water. Turn and baste the pork rack with the reserved marinade after 1 hour and again after 2 hours.

Baste a final time a few minutes before taking the ribs from the grill.

JUST PEACHY RIBS

G eorgia is renowned for its peaches and its pork. Combined in this recipe, the pork and the peaches, here sweet and sour from the addition of cider vinegar, mingle to lend a distinctive accent to the smoked fare quite different from the usual barbecue effect. The bourbon, as typical of Georgia hog roast country as the other main ingredients, doesn't hurt the dish either.

SERVES 3 TO 4

2½- to 3½-pound rack of pork spareribs
1 tablespoon butter
1 medium-size onion, finely chopped
1 to 2 cups peach preserves
1 cup light corn syrup
½ cup cider vinegar
¼ cup bourbon
1 tablespoon Worcestershire sauce
1 tablespoon grated fresh gingerroot
1 teaspoon dry mustard
1 clove garlic, peeled and put through a garlic press

Fire up your smoker before starting any of the other preparations for this dish so the coals will be good and hot by the time you need them. You'll want the smoker preheated to about 220 to 240 degrees F. before putting on the ribs, and they will need to cook for some 5 to 7 hours.

Pat the spareribs dry and let rest at room temperature while you make the sauce.

Melt the butter in a medium-size stainless steel or flameproof ceramic saucepan. Add the onion and sauté gently until golden. Stir in 1 cup of the peach preserves and the corn syrup, vinegar, bourbon, and Worcestershire sauce. Add the ginger, dry mustard, and garlic, making sure the mustard dissolves, leaving no lumps. Blend well and simmer the sauce for about 15 minutes, or until it is thick and spreadable. If it doesn't seem to be thickening properly, add up to 1 cup more peach preserves. Fruit jams and compotes vary a lot in pectin content and so react in sauces in quite different ways.

Once the coals in the smoker are smoldering evenly, add your wet smoking wood to the fire pan and fill the water pan, remembering to use hot water. Put the rack of spareribs on the grill and brush liberally with the sauce. Cover the cooker with its lid and smoke the ribs for 4 to 5 hours at 220 to 240 degrees F. Make sure you check the water pan about halfway through this time and add some more charcoal and wood as well.

After their long smoke, glaze the ribs again, turn them, and glaze the other side. Smoke for 1 to 2 additional hours. About 10 minutes before you pull the ribs from the grill, give them an extra generous slathering of goo on both sides.

ABSOLUT RIBS

T he saturation of our lives with advertisements leads most people to block these intrusions from their perception almost automatically. Occasionally, however, an advertising campaign catches our attention so effectively that it becomes part and parcel of our culture. The striking, often humorous ads for the Swedish vodka Absolut fall into this category, as witness the collections people make of them.

I suppose, in order to make these ribs absolutely Absolut, one should pound them into a bottle shape before smoking them. Personally, I settle for the vodka flavor without the form.

3- to 4-pound rack of pork spareribs
1 cup orange juice
½ cup lime juice
½ cup white vinegar
½ cup sugar
1 teaspoon cornstarch
1 teaspoon dry mustard
1 teaspoon crushed red pepper
2 tablespoons olive oil
½ cup Absolut Citron
1 scallion, greens included, finely chopped
zest of 1 lemon
zest of 1 lime
½ teaspoon salt

A day or two before this dish is to grace the menu, set out a non-reactive bowl or dish deep and wide enough to hold the rack of spareribs easily.

In a medium-size stainless steel or flameproof ceramic saucepan, bring the orange juice, lime juice, and vinegar to a boil. While this mixture is heating, measure the sugar into a small cup and stir in the cornstarch, dry mustard, and crushed red pepper, blending well. Add a little liquid from the saucepan to the dry ingredients, forming a thick paste, then dilute with a little more liquid from the pan, and, finally, stir the thin paste into the liquid in the saucepan. Simmer the mix for about 15 to 20 minutes, or until thick.

Remove the pan from the heat and allow to cool. Then stir in the olive oil, Absolut, scallion, lemon and lime zest, and salt.

Pour a little of the sauce into the bottom of your marinating dish and add the spareribs. Slather the rest of the sauce over the rack of ribs.

Marinate the meat, tightly covered with plastic wrap, in the refrigerator for 1 to 2 days, turning the rack once or twice a day and spooning the extra marinade in the dish over the ribs each time. As you're turning the ribs, pierce them all over with a fork to help the sauce permeate the meat.

About 4½ to 6½ hours before dinnertime, start a fire in the smoker and let it build up a good bed of coals. The spareribs will want a good 4 to 6 hours of smoking at 220 to 240 degrees F. to reach the finger-licking tender stage, although they will be technically done much sooner, when they've reached an internal temperature of 160 to 170 degrees F. Keep plenty of wet wood sizzling in the fire pan and plenty of hot water in the water pan, and keep the lid on the smoker.

And yes, any remaining marinade can be heated and served as a sauce with the ribs. Absolut-ly.

SIMPLE SAUCY RIBS

Recipes tend to grow in complexity over the years as a style of cooking becomes entrenched and each chef tries to add some special culinary signature. Then the siren of simplicity sounds, everything is thrown out, and cooks start over, luring the palate with pure and primary tastes.

Some ribs I've sampled boast as many as thirty separate ingredients in their marinade alone, which surely is overdoing it. Among other things, you're bound to be out of one or another supposedly critical spice halfway through the making of the dish. So here's a very basic rib recipe that yields very good ribs. Purists will no doubt object to the garlic powder, and certainly fresh garlic, either pressed or slivered, can be substituted for it.

SERVES 3 TO 4

2- to 3-pound rack of pork spareribs
½ cup firmly packed dark brown sugar
1 tablespoon garlic powder
1 to 2 teaspoons ground cayenne pepper
1 teaspoon ground coriander
½ cup cider vinegar
1 tablespoon Worcestershire sauce
1 fifteen-ounce can tomato sauce

The day before this rib repast, set the rack of ribs out on a cutting board or butcher block and slice between the ribs one-third of the way in from both ends so that the sauce can work its way in between them. Set aside while you prepare the marinade.

Scoop the brown sugar into a medium-size mixing bowl and press out any lumps with a fork or the back of a spoon. Blend in the garlic powder, cayenne pepper, and coriander. If you like your ribs mild, use the smaller amount of pepper, if very hot, the larger amount. Add the vinegar and Worcestershire sauce to the dry ingredients and stir until smooth, then mix in the tomato sauce and stir again.

Place the spareribs in a large Ziploc-type plastic bag and pour the marinade over them. Seal the bag and knead it between your palms a few times to work the marinade around the ribs. Refrigerate overnight.

Fire up your smoker 6 to 7 hours before you want to serve the ribs. Once the coals have caught well, add wet smoking wood, a pan of hot water, and the grill. Arrange the pork rack on the grill so that the ribs curve upward. Cover the cooker and smoke the ribs at 200 to 240 degrees F. for 2 hours.

After this preliminary smoking, baste the ribs and smoke them for 1 additional hour. Then turn the ribs, baste again, and smoke for 2 to 3 more hours or until you can't wait any longer. Baste them liberally one final time a few minutes before taking them from the smoker.

Serve these simple, choice ribs just as they come from the grill or, for variety, with plenty of your favorite dipping sauce.

HOISIN RIBS

Hoisin sauce has been called the tomato catsup of the Orient. It even looks a bit like catsup, albeit a rather browner version of it. However, hoisin sauce contains no tomatoes, employing instead a fermented soybean base. Added to this base are the same sugar, vinegar, and spices that infuse our catsup. So it's no wonder that the sauce estimably enlivens a rib glaze.

SERVES 3 TO 4

> *3- to 4-pound rack of pork spareribs, separated*
> *1 cup hoisin sauce*
> *½ cup dark corn syrup*
> *½ cup rice vinegar*
> *2 cloves garlic, peeled and put through a garlic press*
> *2 tablespoons sesame seeds*
> *1 teaspoon sesame oil*
> *1 teaspoon ground cayenne pepper*
> *1 teaspoon ground ginger*
> *4 to 6 tablespoons wet tea leaves or 6 tea bags*

The day before you plan to smoke the ribs, lay them out on their sides in a nonreactive glass or ceramic dish large enough to accommodate them together with the marinade.

In a small mixing bowl or pitcher, whisk together the hoisin sauce, corn syrup, and vinegar. Add the garlic, sesame seeds, sesame oil, cayenne pepper, and ginger. Blend well.

Measure half of this mixture into a container suitable for storage, cover tightly, and refrigerate to be used as a dipping sauce for the ribs when served. Pour the other half of the mixture over the ribs and turn them in the liquid to saturate both sides. Cover tightly with plastic wrap and let marinate overnight in the refrigerator.

The ribs will take about 3 hours to cook in a covered smoker kept at an interior temperature of 200 to 240 degrees F., so start the fire about 3½ hours before dinnertime.

When you drain the ribs, save the marinade, pouring it into a small nonreactive saucepan. Heat to a simmer over low heat and set aside to use as a baste.

Before putting the ribs on the grill over their pan of hot water, sprinkle 1 to 2 tablespoons of the wet tea leaves over the coals for smoke in lieu of the more customary soaked wood. Two tea bags will do the job nicely if you have no spent loose tea around. You don't even have to take the tea out of the bags. Just pull off the strings and the tags.

Baste the ribs every 30 minutes or so until they're done, adding more tea to the coals while you're at it.

Serve the ribs with the reserved dipping sauce, reheated until it's piping hot.

BABY BACK RIBS WITH CITRUS

C itrus, be it in the form of oranges, lemons, limes, or even grapefruit, is ideally suited to pork ribs, particularly if they're splashed with a little Worcestershire sauce as well.

SERVES 2 TO 3

> *3- to 4-pound rack of baby back pork ribs, separated*
> *½ cup molasses*
> *¼ cup lime juice*
> *¼ cup lemon juice*
> *¼ cup Worcestershire sauce*
> *zest of 1 lime*
> *zest of 1 lemon*

A day in advance of smoking these ribs, place them in a single layer in a large, shallow dish suitable for marinating. Measure the molasses, lime and lemon juices, and Worcestershire sauce into a small mixing bowl or pitcher. Add the lime and lemon zest and blend well.

Pour the marinade over the ribs, turning them a couple of times to saturate them with the sauce. Cover the dish with plastic wrap and refrigerate overnight.

Start a fire in your smoker about 2½ to 3½ hours before you want to serve the ribs. Then, while the coals are heating, turn your attention to the sauce.

Pour the marinade from the dish of ribs into a small stainless steel or flameproof ceramic saucepan. Simmer the liquid over low heat for 10 to 15 minutes, or until thickened.

By this time, the coals in the smoker should be burning well. Add the wet wood you've chosen for smoke, fill the water pan about halfway with hot water, set it on its supports, and arrange the ribs on the grill. Brush them liberally with sauce, put the lid on the cooker, and smoke for 2 to 3 hours at 200 to 240 degrees F. Turn and baste the ribs after 1 hour and once more after another 30 minutes to 1 hour, by which time they'll be well nigh irresistible.

DR PEPPER RIBS

Coca-Cola and Dr Pepper are both drinks native to the South that made an indelible mark north of the Mason-Dixon line. Coke, around longer, went on to become an international standard-bearer of the American palate. Dr Pepper, on the other hand, has made its way out of Texas only within the past two decades. Northerners haven't yet adopted it as a breakfast drink — which it is for many in Waco, Texas — nor have they embraced it as a culinary ingredient. Still, a lot of barbecue sauces combine the peppery with the sweet, so it should come as no surprise that both Coca-Cola and Dr Pepper are used in cooking down south.

SERVES 4 TO 6

3 to 4 pounds country-style pork ribs
3 cups Dr Pepper, divided
3 cups catsup
1 cup firmly packed dark brown sugar
6 tablespoons chili powder
4 tablespoons ground black pepper
2 tablespoons dry mustard
1 tablespoon ground cinnamon

The day before your country-style cookout, parboil the ribs for 5 minutes to reduce the fat, then drain and let cool.

Transfer the ribs to a large nonreactive glass or ceramic dish and pour 2 cups of the Dr Pepper over them. Reserve the third cup of the soda for a sauce to be made later. Let the ribs marinate, tightly covered with plastic wrap and refrigerated, overnight.

About 6½ hours before you plan to serve the ribs, start a fire in your smoker and begin heating a quantity of coals. Then turn your attention to the sauce.

Pour the remaining 1 cup of Dr Pepper into a blender or food processor and measure in the catsup, brown sugar, chili powder, pepper, dry mustard, and cinnamon. Mix until smooth and well blended — no need to cook this one, at least for now.

Add some well-soaked aromatic wood such as hickory or mesquite to the glowing coals in your smoker, set a pan filled with hot water in place, and smoke the ribs, covered, at 220 to 240 degrees F. for about 3 hours. Don't peek!

After this initial smoking, turn the ribs, slather them with sauce, check the supply of wood and water in their respective pans, and continue cooking for another 3 hours, this time turning the ribs every 30 minutes and mopping them with sauce each time they're turned. By the end of the 3 hours, they should have long since reached the internal temperature of 160 to 170 degrees F. recommended for pork.

After the last basting of the ribs, tote the remaining sauce inside and simmer in a medium-size stainless steel or flameproof ceramic saucepan over low heat until quite thick.

Serve the gloriously gooey sauce in dipping bowls with the finished ribs — with or without a cold Dr Pepper on the side.

GILROY'S GARLIC-GALORE RIBS

For a town to declare itself the garlic capital of the world, as Gilroy, California, did some time ago, would once have been considered public relations suicide. The bad-breath jokes would have gone on endlessly, stretching farther than the flourishing fields of bulbs I viewed on a visit to that town, encircling it as far as the eye could see.

But that was before garlic became aioli and the region of Provence became so prominent in culinary circles, and before it was suggested that garlic could improve everything from your circulation to your love life, its alleged powers depending on the particular proponent of its potency. Today garlic is as common in the American larder as cornflakes. Here, then, is a rib recipe that will leave you, well, breathless.

SERVES 4 TO 6

3 to 4 pounds country-style pork ribs
1 cup red wine vinegar
1 cup water
¼ cup olive oil
2 whole bulbs garlic, the cloves peeled and put through a garlic
    press
1 teaspoon ground white pepper
1 teaspoon Tabasco or similar hot red pepper sauce
½ cup heavy cream
2 tablespoons butter
2 tablespoons flour
½ cup chopped fresh parsley

The day before your planned cookout, parboil the ribs for 5 minutes to reduce the fat layer rimming them. Drain the ribs and let cool.

In a small mixing bowl or pitcher, dilute the vinegar with the water. Add the olive oil, garlic, white pepper, and Tabasco or other hot red pepper sauce. Blend well.

Pour some of the marinade into a nonreactive glass or ceramic dish large enough to hold the ribs. Place the ribs in the liquid and turn them to soak both sides thoroughly. Then pour the rest of the marinade over the ribs. Refrigerate, tightly covered with plastic wrap, overnight. In the morning, turn the ribs and scoop more marinade over them.

About 6 hours or so before dinnertime, preheat your smoker to 200 to 240 degrees F. and add your smoking wood. Drain the ribs, reserving the marinade, and place them on the grill over a filled water pan. Baste them lightly with the reserved marinade, cover the cooker tightly, and let the ribs smoke, undisturbed, for 2 hours.

At the end of that time, turn and lightly baste the ribs again. Let smoke for another 2 hours, making sure that the temperature inside the smoker hovers between 200 and 240 degrees F. and that the water tray remains well supplied.

Turn and baste the ribs once more after they've been on the grill for a total of about 4 hours and smoke them for a final 1 to 2 hours.

Just before serving the ribs, heat the remaining marinade in a medium-size stainless steel or flameproof ceramic saucepan and stir in the cream.

In a separate small frying pan, melt the butter and mix in the flour to form a paste. Spoon a little of the marinade from the saucepan into this roux and stir quickly to keep the mixture smooth as it thickens.

Pour the diluted roux back into the saucepan and blend the sauce until smooth and creamy. Toss in all but a little of the parsley at the last minute and stir lightly a few times.

Arrange the ribs on a platter and pour the hot sauce over them just before serving. Garnish with the bit of reserved parsley.

RIBS À LA UNCLE ROBERT

Most ribs are served smothered in a lusciously gooey, barbecue-red, catsup-based sauce. Now there are some folks, believe it or not, who can't abide catsup, dislike tomatoes intensely, and view with a suspicion worthy of arsenic any remotely red-hued sauce. My Uncle Robert is one of these.

On the other hand, being Austrian, he is by birth a carnivore of considerable consumption. High on his list of favored meats, furthermore, is *Geselchtes,* a term referring, in the Austrian dialect, to smoked fare.

In the *Heurigers,* or wine pubs, around Vienna, *Geselchtes* and other succulent meats are sliced for you on demand from steaming-hot trays and served with a choice of flavorsome breads. Within the past couple of decades, salad bars have even crept onto the scene, albeit remaining modestly in the background. What hasn't made its appearance yet is any form of sauce as we know it to accompany the meat. Mustard and horseradish are the standards in Austrian *Heuriger* cuisine. This recipe puts a tiny chink in that tradition.

SERVES 4 TO 6

3 to 4 pounds country-style pork ribs
1 cup olive oil
1 cup lemon juice
8 cloves garlic, peeled and put through a garlic press
4 tablespoons grated fresh gingerroot
4 tablespoons dry mustard
1 tablespoon prepared horseradish
2 teaspoons ground white pepper
2 teaspoons salt

A day in advance of putting this dish on the menu, parboil the ribs in a large pot for 5 minutes to help reduce the fat layers running through them. Drain the ribs and let cool while you mix up the marinade.

Pour the olive oil and lemon juice into a blender or food processor and mix well. Add the garlic, ginger, dry mustard, horseradish, white pepper, and salt. Blend thoroughly.

Place the ribs in a nonreactive glass or ceramic dish large enough to accommodate them side by side in a single layer and deep enough for them to soak in their marinade. Pour the sauce over them and turn the ribs to coat them well on both sides. Cover with plastic wrap and refrigerate overnight. In the morning, turn the ribs once more.

The ribs will need about 6 hours of smoking at 210 to 240 degrees F., although by that time they should have long since reached and passed the requisite internal temperature of 160 to 170 degrees F. Start heating the smoker about 30 minutes before you want to put the ribs on, and for generating the smoke, use a fragrant fruitwood such as cherry or apple if you have it. Make sure your smoker's water pan is well filled with hot water too.

When you drain the ribs to transfer them to the grill, reserve the marinade. Let the ribs smoke for about 4 hours, undisturbed, beneath the cooker's lid, unless the wood or water below them needs replenishing.

After this initial smoking, turn the ribs and baste them with some of the reserved marinade. Turn and baste them again after 30 minutes. Repeat every 30 minutes until the ribs are done.

Shortly before serving, pour the leftover marinade into a small stainless steel or flameproof ceramic saucepan and simmer for 5 minutes. Transfer to a warmed pitcher or gravy boat from which guests can help themselves. These ribs are not as heavy in flavor as some and make a nice change from tomato-based recipes.

KIMCHI RIBS

S hort ribs, as flavorful as they are, lack the celebrated tenderness of the grander rib cuts from whose periphery they are trimmed. Thus they are ideal candidates for smoke cooking, notable for its tenderizing effect.

Kimchi, the spicy Korean counterpart of a rough-cut sauerkraut accenting these rather mild ribs with such delightful piquancy, is now quite readily available in larger supermarkets as well as in Oriental grocery stores.

SERVES 4

8 beef short ribs, about 4 to 5 pounds total
1 fifteen-ounce jar kimchi

The night before the ribs are to be smoked, parboil them in a large pot for 10 minutes to help tenderize the meat and reduce the fat. Drain the ribs and let cool while you mix up the marinade for them.

Pour the juice from the kimchi into a glass or ceramic dish large enough to hold the ribs. Refrigerate the cabbage itself, tightly sealed in its jar, to keep it moist. Pierce the ribs all over with a sharp fork, lay them in the dish, and turn them over a couple of times to absorb the kimchi juice. Let them marinate, covered and refrigerated, overnight.

About 3½ to 4½ hours before you plan to serve the ribs, fire up your smoker and start a good bed of coals heating.

Drain the ribs lightly and, using a kitchen syringe, inject the remaining kimchi juice into them. The kimchi juice, despite its pungency, will impart a delicate, rather than overwhelming, flavor to the ribs.

Place the ribs, bone side down, on your smoker grill, add wet wood to the fire pan and hot water to the water pan, and smoke the meat, snug under the cooker's lid, for 3 to 4 hours at 200 to 230 degrees F., checking the wood and water levels occasionally.

Serve the short ribs smothered in the reserved kimchi. The dual contrast between the steaming-hot ribs and the cold kimchi and between the crisp, spicy cabbage and the tender, delicately flavored smoky meat really awakens the palate.

RETRO RIBS

Grenadine syrup is one of those pink-lemonade, pink-lady, pink-everything icons of the fifties, that decade so wonderful to behold through the rose-colored glasses of retrospect. So when in the supermarket one day I came across a row of Giroux grenadine bottles, their blue-and-gold labels still proclaiming their contents "Guaranteed Wholesome," I stuck one in my cart along with a flood of memories.

As a child, I associated grenadine with the Caribbean and the archipelago in the Windward Islands whose name it shares. Whether there was some real connection between them I've never discovered. All the same, the ornate, old-fashioned label transported me back to the porches of my youth, where I would sip cool summer refreshers of grenadine with water and ice and dream of sailing under fresh breezes to faraway lands. Images of the grenadine-glazed hams of a distant aunt also came briefly to mind.

For those who like a sweet accompaniment with their meat, the sauce in this recipe is a real taste treat. For those restricting their sodium intake, it also has the advantage of using no salt, a commodity added in considerable quantity to most, and particularly commercial, barbecue sauces.

SERVES 4

8 beef short ribs, about 4 to 5 pounds total
1 cup grenadine syrup
1 cup lime juice
1 cup molasses

As with so many smoked dishes, this one is started a day in advance. The night before you plan to smoke the ribs, parboil them in a large pot for 10 minutes to help tenderize them and reduce the fat. Drain the ribs and let cool while you mix up the marinade for them.

In a glass or ceramic dish large and deep enough to hold the ribs with a bit of space left over, stir the grenadine syrup, lime juice, and molasses together until they are smooth and well blended.

Prick the short ribs well with a fork, lay them in the sauce, and spoon some of the marinade over them. Cover tightly with plastic wrap and refrigerate the dish overnight. In the morning, turn the ribs in their marinade.

Start a good bed of coals in your smoker about 3½ to 4½ hours before you plan to serve the ribs. When the coals are hot, drain the ribs lightly, reserving the marinade, and transfer them to the grill, bone side down.

Smoke the ribs in the lidded cooker for 3 to 4 hours at 210 to 230 degrees F., keeping the pan below them about half full of hot water and checking the supply of wet wood periodically.

About 1 hour before you plan to serve the ribs, simmer the reserved marinade until thick in a medium-size stainless steel or flameproof ceramic saucepan set over low heat. Paint the ribs with this gloriously sticky stuff for their finishing smoke. Glaze the ribs a final time just as you take them from the grill.

COLESLAW

C oleslaw and ribs go together like country and cooking, and there are a zillion variations on the theme. Every recipe has its one secret ingredient. This one has two, chives and horseradish, each adding its own trademark zing to the slaw.

If you can, mix up this slaw up a day or two in advance of the meal where it's to be served. It just gets better (up to a point, of course) with age. If there's not time for the longer resting period, at least put it first in the order of dinner preparations so it will have time to mellow for a few hours.

Attractive made with either the young green, the more mature white, or the red variant of cabbage, coleslaw is even more handsome when a blend of colors is used. The horseradish can be freshly grated, prepared, or in the form of the green-tinted wasabi found in the Oriental section of most supermarkets.

SERVES 4 TO 6

1 small head cabbage, 2 to 3 pounds, or ½ head green or white
and ½ head red cabbage, outer leaves discarded, very finely
shredded
½ small onion, grated
½ cup finely minced fresh chives
2 cups sour cream
¼ cup milk
2 tablespoons grated horseradish or an equal amount of wasabi
mixed with 2 tablespoons water to form a paste
½ teaspoon ground white pepper
salt to taste (optional)

A slaw made with sour cream is more lightly but thoroughly mixed, I've found, if the cabbage is added in installments.

Place a handful or two of the shredded cabbage in a large mixing bowl, add the onion and chives, and toss well.

In a separate small bowl or cup, stir together the sour cream, milk, horseradish or wasabi paste, white pepper, and, if you wish, a sprinkling of salt, although I find that ingredient hardly needed here.

Add part of the dressing to the salad ingredients in the bowl and mix lightly with a fork, then add more shredded cabbage, more dressing, and so on until you have a nicely mixed batch of slaw.

Cover the bowl and refrigerate until you're ready to serve, turning the slaw as it mellows when you happen to think of it. Serve well chilled.

5. QUINTESSENTIAL PORK

A sk a southerner what the quintessential barbecue dish is, and the answer will be pork. There all agreement will end. The best wood to put beneath it — hickory, maple, oak, apple, and some would add pecan — is a topic of considerable debate. Then there's the matter of cooking "dry," with only a spicy rub before smoking, or "wet," mopping a sauce over the meat for the last half hour of cooking and again as it's served, or both. Finally, there's the great controversy over whether to dish the pork up sliced, chunked, or "pulled," as in pulled apart. For me the last debate centers on the cut. A pork shoulder — whether picnic, from the lower section, or butt, from the upper — should definitely be pulled, to my mind. Cutting it just doesn't cut it. The pull should also be served on fluffy white rolls, no sesame seeds, with lots and lots of sauce.

Now before anyone starts writing letters setting me straight on this point, let me reiterate that it's just my opinion. No one has to agree with it. What no one can help agreeing with, though, is that there are no ifs, buts, or maybes when it comes to the delight of a well-mopped bit of smoked pork.

PUSHMI-PULLYU PORK

In barbecue country, even where agreement has been reached on the matter of pulled versus carved pork, the presence or absence of a bone to pull or slice it from may still remain a subject of unresolved, if good-humored, controversy. A minority vote for boneless roast. What's not up for debate is that the meat must be done to the stage where it's literally falling apart.

The recipe given here is a classic three-step one involving rub, mop, and sauce. The result, of course, is perfect pulled pork.

SERVES 10 TO 14

6- to 8-pound Boston pork butt

THE RUB
¼ cup paprika
3 tablespoons coarsely ground black pepper
3 tablespoons chili powder
3 tablespoons ground cumin
3 tablespoons dry mustard
2 tablespoons dark brown sugar
1 tablespoon ground cayenne pepper
1 teaspoon salt

THE MOP
2 cups cider vinegar
½ cup water
2 tablespoons dark brown sugar
1 tablespoon Worcestershire sauce
1 tablespoon Tabasco or similar hot red pepper sauce
1 tablespoon crushed red pepper

THE SAUCE

3 tablespoons corn oil
2 medium-size onions, chopped
1½ cups cider vinegar
1½ cups catsup
¼ cup molasses
¼ cup firmly packed dark brown sugar
2 tablespoons paprika
1 tablespoon dry mustard
1 teaspoon crushed red pepper
1 teaspoon ground cayenne pepper

THE ACCOMPANIMENT

fluffy white hamburger buns

Pulled pork traditionally reposes in its rub overnight. So the day before it's to be smoked, set out the roast, pat it dry with a paper towel, and let it rest at room temperature while you collect the spices for it.

Measure into a small mixing bowl the paprika, black pepper, chili powder, cumin, dry mustard, brown sugar, cayenne pepper, and salt. Stir the spices until well blended and free of clumps.

Rub the pork butt all over with half of the rub. Set aside the other half, tightly covered, in its bowl. Refrigerate the roast overnight in a sealed Ziploc-type plastic bag.

The following day, take the pork butt from the refrigerator and work the reserved rub into it. Let the roast rest in its coating of spices while you build a fire in your smoker and get a good set of coals going. Do this early. You should plan on up to 9 hours' smoking time from start to finish for this dish.

Next, make the mop, or basting sauce, for the pork. Pour the vinegar and water into a medium-size stainless steel or flameproof ceramic saucepan. Add the brown sugar, Worcestershire sauce, Tabasco or other hot red pepper sauce, and crushed red pepper. Stir until well blended. Heat briefly before using, or simply place the pan, covered, by the hot smoker to stay warm until needed.

As soon as the smoker has reached a temperature of 200 to 220 degrees F., add a liberal supply of wet wood to the fire pan and hot water to the water pan.

Baste the pork butt generously with the mop and put it on to smoke, covered by the cooker's lid, for 6 to 8 hours, keeping the temperature between 200 to 220 degrees F., replenishing the wood and water pans as needed, and mopping the butt at 1-hour intervals. You want it falling-apart tender.

When the pork seems near perfection, start the sauce to serve with it.

In a fairly large stainless steel or flameproof ceramic saucepan, heat the corn oil. Add the onion and sauté over medium heat until golden. Add the vinegar, catsup, molasses, and brown sugar, and blend until smooth. Sprinkle in the paprika, dry mustard, and crushed red and cayenne peppers, whisking to forestall clumping. Simmer the sauce for 10 minutes, stirring occasionally. Keep warm.

Remove the pork butt from the grill and let it cool on a platter for about 20 minutes or until, purists would say, you can pull the meat apart with your hands without being burned. Whether with hands or forks, shred the meat as you pull. If you're of a more puritan school of barbecue etiquette, you can carve the meat instead, chopping it as you go.

In any case, serve it heaped on a platter with appropriately decadent air-filled fluffy white buns and a large pitcher of the warm sauce. Don't pour the sauce over the pork on the platter. If you do, the meat will become as soggy as sloppy joe, a different dish altogether. The sauce, often called a finishing sauce, is poured over the meat after it's piled onto the bottom half of its bun, at the very last minute before the top goes on. It should ooze out the sides of the sandwich every time you take a bite.

FOIL-WRAPPED PORK BUTT

n this recipe, the pork is "finished" wrapped in foil for the last hour of its long smoke. Normally, to my mind such foil wrapping would fall into the cheating category, but one can't be a purist all the time. The foil in this case is needed to keep the onion slices and juices nestled around the butt. Besides, the meat is so tender by the time it's bundled up that without the foil, it would fall right through the grill.

SERVES 6 TO 8

3- to 4-pound boneless pork butt

THE RUB
½ cup firmly packed dark brown sugar
3 tablespoons paprika
3 tablespoons ground black pepper
2 tablespoons ground white pepper
2 tablespoons garlic powder
2 tablespoons dry mustard
1 tablespoon ground cayenne pepper
1 tablespoon salt

THE MOP
½ of the rub
1 cup cider vinegar
1 cup very strong coffee
½ cup honey
1 medium-size onion, minced

THE FINISH
1 medium-size onion, sliced
extra mop

THE ACCOMPANIMENT
fluffy white hamburger buns

At least a day — two doesn't hurt — before your planned barbecue, pat the pork butt dry with a paper towel and place it on a large ceramic platter or in a shallow glass or stainless steel pan.

In a small mixing bowl, mash the brown sugar briefly with a fork to crumble any lumps left from packing it into its measuring cup. Stir in the paprika, black and white peppers, garlic powder, dry mustard, cayenne pepper, and salt. Mix until thoroughly blended.

Divide the seasoning mixture into two portions and set one aside, tightly covered. Rub the remaining seasoning into the pork. Place the butt in a Ziploc-type plastic bag, seal, and refrigerate for 1 to 2 days.

Some 7 to 9 hours before your barbecue dinner, the time depending more or less on the size of the pork butt, remove the meat from the refrigerator and allow it to stand at room temperature.

Start a fire in the smoker a couple of hours after you've set out the pork butt. While the smoker is heating, prepare the mop.

Place the extra seasoning ingredients set aside earlier in a small stainless steel or flameproof ceramic saucepan, add a little of the vinegar, and stir to a smooth paste. Then pour in the rest of the vinegar and add the coffee, honey, and onion. Blend the ingredients and warm the mixture over low heat, stirring constantly, until it begins to bubble. Set aside until needed for basting.

Place the pork on the grill of your smoker over wet wood and a pan of hot water, cover the cooker, and smoke at 200 to 220 degrees F. for 4½ to 6 hours, or until a meat thermometer registers an internal temperature of 160 to 170 degrees F., mopping the meat with some of the basting liquid at 1-hour intervals and checking the wood and water supplies while the cover is off the smoker.

For the finish, when the pork is done, lay out across a platter a piece of heavy-duty aluminum foil large enough to enclose the butt. Spread the onion slices in a rough circle in the middle of the foil and transfer the pork from the grill to the bed of onion. Pour the remaining mop over the butt, fold over and seal the edges of the foil securely, and return the wrapped butt to the grill.

Smoke for 1 additional hour, adding extra coals to the fire to bring the temperature of the smoker up to 250 degrees F. By the end of the hour, the internal temperature of the meat should have reached some 190 degrees F. This finish is what puts the pork into the falling-apart category.

Once you've removed the butt from the smoker, open the foil and, if you possibly can, let the pork rest for 10 to 15 minutes before serving with the customary soft buns. I should warn you, however, that the aroma may prove irresistible long before the suggested waiting time is up.

THE PERFECT PICNIC

P icnic pork shoulder comes "as is," referring to the bone-in cut, or boneless, skinless, rolled, and tied. Either of the above can be used in this recipe. Myself, I prefer a bone-in picnic. If the meat nearest the bone is the sweetest, as the old saying goes, then surely it's sweetest of all when cooked while the bone is still there.

This recipe makes finger-licking, falling-off-the-bone-tender pulled pork perfect for serving either on the traditional soft buns or plain. Dish up plenty of extra vinegar sauce.

SERVES 8 TO 10

6- to 7-pound picnic pork shoulder, preferably bone-in

THE RUB
⅓ cup firmly packed dark brown sugar
2 tablespoons garlic powder
2 tablespoons paprika
2 tablespoons ground white pepper
2 tablespoons ground black pepper
1 tablespoon ground cayenne pepper
1 tablespoon dry mustard
2 teaspoons ground sage
2 teaspoons ground thyme
1 teaspoon ground allspice

THE MOP AND SAUCE
2 cups cider vinegar
1 cup corn oil
1 tablespoon Tabasco or similar hot red pepper sauce

THE ACCOMPANIMENT
fluffy white hamburger buns

The day before you want to serve this dish, set out a Ziploc-type plastic bag large enough to hold the pork shoulder. Measure into the bag the rub ingredients: brown sugar; garlic powder; paprika; white, black, and cayenne peppers; dry mustard; sage; thyme; and allspice. Close the bag and shake the contents to mix the spices well, pressing out any clumps of brown sugar between your fingers.

Pat the pork shoulder dry with a paper towel and place it in the bag. Seal the bag, then shake and turn it until the meat is well covered with the rub. Refrigerate, tightly closed, overnight.

Some 8 or 9 hours before you want to eat, take the pork in its bag of spices from the refrigerator and let it rest at room temperature while you fire up the smoker. Once the coals are glowing and you've added smoking wood to the fire pan and hot water to the water pan, transfer the picnic shoulder to the grill.

Smoke, covered, at 200 to 220 degrees F. for 3 to 4 hours, replenishing the cooker's wood and water supplies as needed. Then prepare to start mopping.

Pour the vinegar, corn oil, and Tabasco or other hot red pepper sauce into a medium-size stainless steel or flameproof ceramic saucepan and whisk until well mixed. Baste the shoulder with the mop, using a long-handled barbecue brush or a mop. If you're cooking a bone-in shoulder, be sure to work the mop in around the bone where the meat has begun to separate from it.

Continue to smoke the picnic for another 4 to 5 hours, mopping the crusty black surface every 30 minutes or so. A meat thermometer inserted into the thickest part of the shoulder will have long since registered the 160 to 170 degrees F. recommended for pork, and by now, you'll find, the meat can be pulled apart into luscious, incredibly tender strands all peppery around the edges.

Just before taking the shoulder from the grill, bring the liquid remaining from the mop to a boil in its pan, simmer briefly, and pour into a pitcher to pass around the table. Some folks like their pulled pork really vinegary.

Have soft buns handy for purists.

SMOKED PORK ROAST WITH *PIRIPIRI*

There's something exceptionally satisfying about a substantial pork roast set out as a cookout centerpiece, keeping both the nibbling and the conversation going while a summer evening stretches slowly into dusk. Here's a dish to linger over for a long time.

Hot peppers are much relished by the Portuguese, whose tastes have no doubt been influenced by their country's long association with Brazil. *Piripiri* epitomizes this predilection of the Portuguese palate, being nothing, really, but chili peppers steeped in olive oil. The contrast between the mild, smoky, sweet pork and the hot *piripiri* is adjustable. Some folks like the merest suggestion of sauce with their roast. Others prefer their pork covered in fire.

In considering this dish for a particular day's menu, bear in mind that *piripiri* needs to steep for a couple of days to bring out its flavor — mellow would be the wrong word here. So you'll need to make it up in advance. (The simple recipe follows that for the pork.)

This plain smoked roast lends itself especially well to experimentation with different condiments. Besides *piripiri,* it can be served with a whole palette of accompaniments so diners can select a different one when they come back for seconds. (For ideas, see the chapter devoted to sauces.)

SERVES 4 TO 6

3½- to 4½-pound boneless pork loin, rolled and tied
8 cloves garlic, peeled and slivered
olive oil
1 tablespoon coarsely ground black pepper
1 tablespoon paprika
1 teaspoon salt

Start your preparations for smoking the loin some 4½ to 5½ hours before dinnertime, lighting a fire in your smoker and adding a liberal supply of coals.

With a skewer or a sharp-pointed knife, pierce the entire surface of the pork loin at intervals of about 1 inch, inserting a sliver of garlic into each slit as you go. Then brush the meat lightly with olive oil.

In a small mixing bowl, combine the pepper, paprika, and salt. Sprinkle the mixture over the pork and pat evenly.

Add some wet wood to the smoker's fire pan and hot water to the water pan. When the smoke is billowing, transfer the roast to the grill, cover the smoker, and cook the loin at 200 to 230 degrees F. for 4 to 5 hours, lifting the lid only to check quickly on the water and wood supplies. By the end of the long smoke, a meat thermometer inserted into the thickest part of the roast should have long since registered 160 to 170 degrees F., and the roast will be tender and sweet.

Serve the *piripiri* separately and let guests choose their punishment.

PIRIPIRI

For a proper *piripiri,* you'll need a dozen very hot — not medium, not mild — dried peppers of a variety such as Piquin, Thai, or cayenne.

> *1 cup olive oil*
> *12 dried hot peppers, stemmed*

Pour the olive oil into a small nonreactive saucepan and warm it over medium heat to 300 degrees F. Using a candy thermometer to monitor its progress will prevent you from burning the oil.

Remove the pan from the heat and add the peppers. Set aside to cool.

Once the oil has reached room temperature, pour it, complete with the peppers, into a jar. Cover tightly and let the peppers steep for at least 2 days. Then strain the oil into a cruet. You won't want to use any large quantities of this oil without tasting it first.

PRUNE-STUFFED PORK LOIN

P ork and prunes are a classic European culinary combination that lends itself marvelously to smoke cooking. The prunes add extra moisture and flavor to the meat, while visually the dark fruit contrasts grandly with the light pork.

Add a couple of onions and a carrot to the water when smoking a pork roast. Between the vegetables and the drippings, you'll have an excellent base for a flavorsome gravy.

SERVES 4 TO 6

3½- to 4½-pound boneless pork loin, rolled and tied
1½ cups pitted prunes
1 tablespoon dark brown sugar
1 tablespoon garlic powder
1 tablespoon ground allspice
1 teaspoon ground nutmeg
1 teaspoon ground thyme
1 teaspoon ground cayenne pepper
2 small onions
1 large carrot
2 teaspoons cornstarch
3 tablespoons sour cream
3 tablespoons red currant jelly

This pork roast is best stuffed and spiced the evening before you plan to roast it.

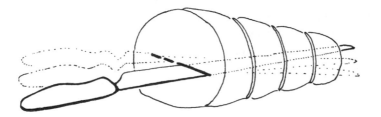

Lay the roast on a cutting board, pat it dry with a paper towel, and work a long, fairly broad, sharp knife through its core. What you want is a tunnel through the center of the roast. Cut horizontally first, then vertically, making an **X** the entire length of the roast. Take care not to cut through to the outside of the roast.

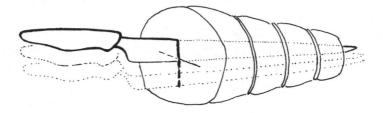

Stuff the cavity you've made with as many prunes as will fit, working first from one end and then from the other. The roast will look round and plump.

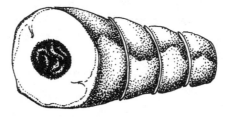

In a Ziploc-type plastic bag large enough to hold the loin, shake together the brown sugar, garlic powder, allspice, nutmeg, thyme, and cayenne pepper, making sure all the lumps are worked out of the brown sugar. Put the roast in the bag and roll it in the spice mix, coating it well and pressing the seasoning into it. Refrigerate the roast, sealed in its bag, overnight.

The following day, build up the fire in your smoker 6 to 7 hours in advance of your dinner hour to provide time for the roast to cook leisurely. Also, for this dish, be sure the smoker's water pan is well scrubbed, and line it with aluminum foil. You'll be using its contents for stock.

When the smoker is hot, add wet wood and hot water to their respective pans and put the loin on to cook at 210 to 230 degrees F. for 4 to 5 hours, or until it reaches an internal temperature of 160 to 170 degrees F., plus 1 more hour to mellow the prunes to delectable succulence.

The water and wood levels in the smoker will both need to be checked periodically during the long, slow cooking of this dish. During one of these checks about halfway into the smoking process, when you'll have the lid off the smoker anyhow, gently drop the onions and the carrot into the water pan to cook with the drippings from the roast for a gravy base. To that same end, let the water level in the pan reduce to about 2 cups toward the end of the smoking period.

About 10 minutes before serving the loin, pour the 2 cups of liquid from the water pan into a medium-size stainless steel or flameproof ceramic saucepan, straining out and discarding the vegetables. Set the saucepan on the stove over high heat and bring the liquid to a rapid boil.

Mix the cornstarch with a little cold water, reduce the heat beneath the stock, and add the cornstarch to the gravy, stirring until smooth. Simmer for 2 to 3 minutes, or until the gravy is thick. Add the sour cream and jelly and blend until creamy. Serve as an accompaniment to the pork loin.

PORK PECAN ROLL WITH MAPLE SAUCE

C oming from Europe, I was familiar with hazelnuts from early childhood on. Pecans, on the other hand, might as well have been extraterrestrial, for all I knew. I first discovered them when Susan, my college steady and now wife, baked me a large and generously filled pecan pie. I had a slice and then, overcome with enthusiasm, seconds. A while later, I went back for more. Before the evening was out, I had drunk half a gallon of milk and eaten the whole thing!

My passion for pecans, particularly in pie form, has not diminished. My input, wisely enough, has.

This early encounter with pecans led to my associating the nuts with things sweet, a connection continuing in my mind to this day. Now the fact that Chappie Rich of We-Li-Kit Farm, up the road a ways, taps our maple grove in exchange for a copious supply of syrup from his sugarhouse means that in our family the sweetener of choice for pies, ice cream sundaes, and even pork roast is maple syrup — which is how this recipe came about.

SERVES 5 TO 8

4- to 6-pound boneless pork loin
2 tablespoons butter
2 medium-size onions, finely chopped
2 cups pecans, coarsely chopped
1½ cups maple syrup
½ cup catsup
½ cup cider vinegar
¼ cup lemon juice
2 tablespoons olive oil
2 teaspoons grated lemon zest
½ teaspoon Tabasco or similar hot red pepper sauce
½ cup minced fresh parsley

If you procured your pork loin from the supermarket — from a butcher it can be bought cut to order — chances are it came rolled and tied. Assuming it did, the night before putting this dish on the menu, take out the loin and unroll it, the better to stuff it later. Return it to the refrigerator, covered, in its flattened state. Then turn your attention to what will be the stuffing.

Melt the butter in a small frying pan, add the onion, and sauté until golden.

Transfer the sautéed onion to a medium-size mixing bowl and add the chopped pecans. Swirl these two ingredients together to mix well, then add the maple syrup, catsup, vinegar, lemon juice, olive oil, lemon zest, and Tabasco or other hot red pepper sauce. Blend well, cover with plastic wrap, and set aside overnight, unrefrigerated, to soften the pecans and let them absorb the other flavors.

About 5½ to 6½ hours before dinnertime, drain the pecans and onion by pouring the sauce through a sieve into another bowl. Since the liquid will be quite thick and sticky, this will take a bit of time. So while you're waiting, fire up your smoker and start a good bed of coals.

Cut a few lengths of untreated cotton cord and lay them out approximately 1½ inches apart on a cutting board. Place the pork loin lengthwise on top of the string.

Spoon the drained pecans and onion in a row down the center of the roast, then sprinkle the parsley over them. Roll the loin up lengthwise with the dressing inside and tie the roll securely. Reserve the strained sauce to use as a baste.

Add some wet wood to your smoker's fire pan and fill the water pan halfway with hot water. Lay the stuffed roast on the grill and mop generously with the reserved sauce before putting the lid on the cooker.

Smoke the loin for 5 to 6 hours, basting every 45 minutes or so. By that time, it should have long since passed the recommended internal temperature of 160 to 170 degrees F. You want the pork tender and moist on the inside, gooey and lusciously dark on the outside.

KASSELER RIPPCHEN

K asseler *Rippchen* is a five-star winner in German cuisine. Whether or not the dish was created in the town of Kassel, which lies between Frankfurt and Hannover, by a Berlin butcher also named Kassel stands as much chance of resolution as the question of who it was that served the first hamburger on a bun. In any event, this smoked pork loin is found throughout Germany.

The loin may be whole or it may be separated into chops. Chops are the usual form it takes when combined with sauerkraut.

One of the unusual aspects of *Kasseler Rippchen* is that the pork is first smoked and then cooked all over again. (So is a ham, of course, in the usual way of things, but the final result there is altogether different.) In the conventional preparation of this dish, the pork is baked in the oven following its preliminary smoke. Here, the pork is smoked, provided with all the trimmings for the right flavor meld, then simply returned to the smoker to reach its maximum *Saftigkeit,* or succulence.

The baking pan used for the second round of smoking will tend to become quite blackened in your smoker, although the damage can be contained somewhat by an aluminum foil shield. Also, the total cooking time for the dish will be fractionally longer than it would be if the final baking were done in a conventional oven. On the other hand, the kitchen will remain cool and undisturbed. Besides, the lower heat of the smoker and the steam from its water pan will guarantee that the meat will stay moist and flavorsome and will indeed reach its celebrated *Saftigkeit.*

½ *pork loin comprising 4 to 5 chops, about 3 to 4 pounds total, or 4 separate center-cut pork loin chops, each 1 to 1½ inches thick*

1 *pound fresh or canned sauerkraut, drained*

2 *tablespoons lard or butter*

1 *medium-size onion, coarsely diced*

2 *tart cooking apples such as Granny Smiths, pared, cored, and diced*

1½ *pounds potatoes*

1 *teaspoon black peppercorns*

1 *cup beef stock or 1 beef bouillon cube dissolved in 1 cup boiling water*

½ *cup dry white wine*

Your smoker will be putting in an 8-hour day on this one if you're cooking the pork as a roast — for individual chops you can take a couple of hours off that time — so start a fire early. Make certain that you have a good supply of wet wood or chips on hand. For real honest-to-goodness *Kasseler Rippchen*, you want copious smoke.

When the smoker is billowing smartly at 210 to 230 degrees F., place the chops or loin on the grill as is — no salt, no pepper, nothing. Cover the cooker and smoke the pork for 3 to 4 hours if it's separate chops, 6 hours if a loin. The meat should reach an internal temperature of 160 to 170 degrees F.

Toward the end of this first smoking period, scoop the sauerkraut into a stainless steel or porcelain colander and set aside to drain.

Melt the lard or butter in a small frying pan, add the onion and apple, and sauté until the onion is translucent and the apple has browned a bit.

Peel the potatoes and slice all but one into ½-inch-thick rounds. Grate the last potato, destined for the sauce, and set aside in a small bowl of water to cover.

Remove the pork from the smoker, replacing the lid on the cooker so it will stay hot, and bring the meat inside. If what you've been smoking is a loin, let it rest for a few moments, then cut it gently into chops.

Set out a large ovenproof casserole or nonreactive baking pan and grease it lightly. Scoop half of the drained sauerkraut into the pan and smooth it out into an even layer. Spread the sautéed onion and apple over the sauerkraut. Then lay about half of the potato slices in a thick layer over the onion and apple and sprinkle with the peppercorns. Add the rest of the potato slices followed by the remaining sauerkraut.

Nestle the pork chops in this top layer of kraut, not covering them but submerging the sides completely.

In a small stainless steel or flameproof ceramic saucepan, stir together the beef stock or bouillon, the wine, and the reserved grated potato, well-drained. Heat to a simmer and pour over the pork and sauerkraut.

To help prevent sooting up your casserole or baking pan — almost an inevitability in the smoker if preventive measures are not taken — cut a piece of heavy-duty aluminum foil a little larger than the pan, place the casserole on it, and fold the edges of the foil up around the sides of the pan.

Place the dish in the smoker — don't cover the dish, but do cover the smoker — and let cook for 1½ hours at 220 to 240 degrees F. (Alternatively, cover the casserole tightly — with its own lid if it has one, with aluminum foil if it hasn't — and pop it into your conventional oven to bake at 375 degrees F. for 45 minutes to 1 hour.)

This is a great dish for fall, when the weather is turning and the evenings are cool. There's a hint in it of the heartiness one looks for in winter cooking.

SMOKED PORK CHOPS 'N' BEANS

Beans are a hearty traditional northern staple. Dried legumes early made their culinary mark on both sides of the Atlantic, engendering such regional specialties as the now ubiquitous Boston baked beans, the celebrated cassoulets of Languedoc so redolent of sausage or lamb or goose, and the yellow-pea soup of Scandinavia that's oh-so-satisfying on a cold winter's eve. What all of these culinary variants have in common, besides the legumes, is their dependence on long, slow cooking to meld the flavors of the individual ingredients making up the dish. Thus they are all ideal candidates for smoke cooking.

This recipe accommodates both the northern propensity for seasoning a whole mess of beans with one walnut-size piece of bacon or fatback and the southern preference for a whole plate of pork with just a spoonful of beans on the side.

SERVES 6

6 boneless center-cut pork loin chops, 2 to 2½ pounds total
1 sixteen-ounce package dried pink or small white navy beans
1 medium-size onion, finely chopped
1 small green bell pepper, finely chopped
1 cup molasses
1 cup catsup
1 tablespoon dry mustard
1 teaspoon cider vinegar
1½ cups bean water, drained from the beans after cooking
1 strip bacon
freshly ground black pepper to taste

If the pork chops have a very thick rim of fat around them, trim them lightly. Otherwise leave the fat layer intact, as it will moisten the beans during smoking, leaving the chops themselves lean but tasty. Refrigerate the chops until needed.

The day before you plan to serve this dish, rinse and drain the beans. Place them in a large stainless steel pot and run cold water over them to cover well, removing any beans that float. The beans will swell, so make sure there's at least an inch or so of liquid above them when you start. Soak the beans overnight.

The following morning, bring the beans to a boil in the water in which they were soaked, adding more liquid as needed to cover. With a slotted spoon, skim off the foam that froths to the top when they come to a boil and simmer them uncovered for 1½ to 2 hours, or until tender. The cooking time will vary depending on the variety of beans you use. You want them soft enough to be easily mashed, but still firm enough to hold their shape. You don't want mush.

As soon as the beans are tender, fire up your smoker and get a good steady bed of coals going.

Drain the beans, reserving the cooking water, and return them to the pot. Add the onion, green pepper, molasses, and catsup. Mix well.

In a small cup, make a paste of the dry mustard and vinegar, stirring until there are no lumps. Pour a little of the reserved bean water into the cup to liquefy the paste, then pour the diluted mustard solution into the remaining bean water and mix until smooth. Add the bean liquid to the bean pot and blend.

In a small pan, fry the bacon until soft and translucent. Place both the bacon strip and the fat from the pan in the bottom of a 3-quart Pyrex or similar ovenproof ceramic baking dish measuring about 13 by 9 by 2 inches. That may seem a somewhat odd shape for baked beans, a round covered casserole being considerably more traditional. However, in this case you want room to lay the pork chops out on top of the beans without crowding them, and you want to maximize the surface area of both chops and beans exposed to the flavor-enhancing smoke wafting from the fire pan.

Push the bacon around in the baking dish until the sides are greased as well as the bottom. Leaving the strip in the dish, pour in the beans. Float the pork chops on top of the beans, sprinkling them with freshly ground pepper once they're in place.

Line the grill of your smoker with a piece of aluminum foil the size of your baking dish before putting the beans on to smoke. This will make doing the dishes a lot easier later, as it will prevent the rising smoke from blackening the outside of the dish campfire fashion. Set the bean dish on the foil and cover the smoker but not the dish itself.

Smoke the pork and beans at 180 to 210 degrees F., keeping the water pan filled halfway with hot water and the fire pan supplied with wet wood, for 6 to 8 hours, or until the aroma of the dish has become irresistible.

CHILI CHOPS

In tropical countries, chili peppers are the most popular of all condiments, used in one form or another to season dishes ranging from the curries of India to the falafel of North Africa to the fiery pepper sauces of the West Indies. One reason for the chilies' widespread popularity in tropical climes is that they raise the body temperature of those ingesting them, producing perspiration. This makes the surrounding atmosphere seem cool by comparison. No doubt that's why the peppers are so prevalent in barbecue sauces, emblematic of hot-weather fare. Here, then, is a recipe for hot chops to serve on a warm summer's eve.

Chili powder, concocted by the Aztecs sometime before the 1500s, early became a signature ingredient of Mexican dishes. The seasoning is actually a blend of ground chilies, cumin, oregano, garlic, and sometimes other herbs and spices as well, all depending on who's making it and what's handy.

SERVES 4 TO 6

4 to 6 thick center-cut pork loin chops, about ¾ pound each
4 tablespoons chili powder
1 teaspoon ground coriander
1 teaspoon ground black pepper
olive oil

About 3 to 4 hours before these chops are to be served, pat them dry with a paper towel, then lay them on a shallow platter.

In a small bowl, stir the chili powder, coriander, and pepper together until well blended. Dust this mixture over the chops, turn them, and dust the other side. Stack the chops one on top of the other and let them absorb the spices while you start the smoker.

Once the coals are glowing, add wet smoking wood to the fire pan and hot water to the water pan and set the grill in place. Pour some olive oil onto the platter next to the stack of chops. Swirl a chop in the oil, first one side of it and then the other, let the excess oil drip off, and place the chop on the grill. Repeat with the other chops. Pour the extra olive oil, by then spiced with some of the rub shaken loose from the pork, into the smoker's water pan for extra flavor before putting the lid on the cooker.

Smoke the chops at 210 to 230 degrees F. for 2 to 3 hours, or until cooked to an internal temperature of 160 to 170 degrees F.

We like these chops with plenty of rice. The contrast between the spicy chops and the mild grain makes for a toothsome dish.

PORK CHOPS ZING

Pork chops rank second only to ribs in popularity as barbecue fare. One argument in their favor is that they're easily adjusted to the number of people to be fed. It doesn't much matter whether you're cooking for two, four, or five, since you can plan on one or two chops, depending on their size, per person. A rack of ribs is not so accommodating.

Chops are meatier than ribs, too, another point in their favor. Furthermore, they can be stuffed. Dressings add contrast as well as visual and gustatory surprise to otherwise simple dishes, so it's not remarkable that the stuffing of meats, an ancient culinary art, is presently undergoing a cordial revival.

What follows is a recipe for rice-stuffed chops that incorporates the vinegary zing so popular with pork in the Carolinas. I'd suggest using double-rib chops. Single chops are generally too thin to be stuffed to my satisfaction.

Ribs are sometimes available prepocketed at butcher shops and supermarket meat counters. If they are, buy them that way and save yourself one step in the preparation of this dish.

SERVES 4

4 double-rib center-cut pork loin chops, about 4 to 5 pounds
    total, pocketed if available

THE STUFFING
4 tablespoons butter
1 medium-size onion, minced
2 cups cooked brown rice
2 tablespoons lemon zest
2 tablespoons minced fresh cilantro
2 teaspoons ground white pepper
1 egg

THE BASTE

1 cup molasses
1 cup cider vinegar
2 tablespoons tomato paste
2 teaspoons ground cayenne pepper
2 teaspoons ground allspice
2 teaspoons ground thyme
1 teaspoon ground sage

About 5 hours before dinnertime, fire up the smoker, and while a bed of coals is forming, prepare the chops.

If the ones you bought did not come ready for stuffing, cut a large pocket with a very small hole in each of them by inserting a knife at one edge, working it in a semicircle inside the chop, then withdrawing the blade, flipping the knife, and repeating for the other side — or should I say inside — of the chop. What you want is a nice big cave with just a teaspoon-size entrance.

For the stuffing, melt the butter in a small saucepan set over low heat. Add the onion and sauté until soft and translucent. Then add the rice and toss to mix. Turn off the heat and stir in the lemon zest, cilantro, and white pepper.

Break the egg into a small mixing bowl and beat until smooth. Stir into the rice mixture. Set aside to cool a bit while you make the baste.

In a small stainless steel or flameproof ceramic saucepan, combine the molasses, vinegar, and tomato paste. Blend well, then whisk in the cayenne pepper, allspice, thyme, and sage, making sure any clumps of spices are dissolved. Heat to a simmer and remove from the stove.

Stuff each chop with one-quarter of the rice dressing and press the small opening closed around it. If it won't stay shut, you can secure it with a bamboo or poultry-lacing skewer, but in that case don't forget to remove the fastener before serving.

Add wet wood to your smoker's fire pan and hot water to the water pan. Brush one side of each chop well with the basting sauce before placing it on the grill, sauced side down.

Brush the other side of the chops well, put the lid on the smoker, and leave the chops to cook for 4 hours at 220 to 240 degrees F., disturbing them only to turn and brush them with sauce at 1-hour intervals. By the end of the 4 hours, they should have long since reached the recommended internal temperature of 160 to 170 degrees F. and be fragrant and tender.

CRUSTY CROWN ROAST

Thanks to the retro nineties, that dinner entertaining centerpiece of the fifties, the crown roast, is back, and I for one am glad of it. Simple to prepare, spectacular to contemplate, and too big for a small family to consume alone, it's the perfect excuse for a gathering of friends.

The disappearance of crown roasts — usually pork, but sometimes lamb — from menus countrywide can be attributed to the vanishing of local butchers as the supermarket tsunami swept over the land, completely altering the topography of food retailing. The comeback of these roasts can be ascribed to that same wave, for as the superstore chains have run out of territorial domains to conquer, they've had no choice but to channel their expansion back into specialty marketing, a phenomenon affecting almost every department. Meat counters aren't staffed with butchers in the old, skilled sense of that occupation, but employees are now trained in the preparation of higher-markup items. Among these are the crown roasts.

Speaking of markup, you'll save a bundle if you order your crown roast — it does usually need to be ordered — without the center dressing. It can be stuffed for you, but then it will be weighed in its new and improved entirety, and you'll be charged for the whole package at the price per pound of the chops. Better to buy ground meat for the stuffing separately, at probably half the per-pound cost of chops.

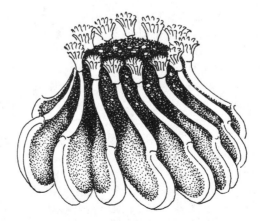

In placing your order, also request that the crown roast be made from center chops, of which there are six or seven to a rack. This will require the butcher to use two racks of chops rather than one in creating a medium-size 12- to 14-bone crown. However, it will also assure you of uniform-size chops. If you're going to serve a crown roast for a company dinner, the last thing you want is a lopsided coronet.

SERVES 8 TO 10

12- to 14-chop crown roast of pork, about 6½ to 7½ pounds

THE STUFFING
¾ pound ground beef
¾ pound ground pork
1 teaspoon ground allspice
1 teaspoon ground black pepper
½ teaspoon ground thyme
½ teaspoon salt
¾ cup pine nuts
½ cup diced dried apricots
½ cup diced pitted prunes

THE MOP
1 egg
2 tablespoons dark brown sugar
2 tablespoons flour
6 cloves garlic, peeled and put through a garlic press
¼ cup prepared whole-grain mustard
¼ cup olive oil
2 teaspoons ground thyme
1 teaspoon ground sage
1 teaspoon ground coriander
1 teaspoon ground white pepper

About 7 to 8 hours before dinnertime, start a fire in your smoker and begin building up a good bed of coals, for this will be a long smoke.

Set the crown roast out on a sturdy platter to support it as it's stuffed.

In a medium-size mixing bowl, blend the ground beef and pork lightly with a fork. Shake the allspice, pepper, thyme, and salt over the meat mixture and blend again to incorporate the spices evenly. Then scatter the pine nuts, apricots, and prunes over the meat and gently fold in.

The stuffing will look as though it won't all fit into the crown roast, but it will, honest. Press the mix down in the center hole until it's just even with the tops of the meaty portion of the chops, leaving the bare bones sticking up around it. Besides adding its own flavor to the roast, the tightly packed stuffing will help the crown to hold its shape.

For the mop, whisk the egg, brown sugar, and flour together in your mixing bowl until well blended and free of lumps. Add the pressed garlic and mustard and blend again. Repeat with the olive oil, then sprinkle in the thyme, sage, coriander, and white pepper. Continue whisking until the liquid is thick and smooth.

Paint the entire outside of the crown roast, including the top of the stuffing, with the mop. Brush plenty of the liquid over the exposed lower portion of the chops between the bones. Reserve the extra mop for a quick finishing baste when the roast is almost done.

Add some wet wood to the coals in your smoker's fire pan and some hot water to the water pan, then transfer the dressed roast to the grill.

Smoke at 190 to 220 degrees F. for 6 to 7 hours, lifting the lid of the cooker only to check the water and wood supplies, at which point you can also check how the roast is progressing. If you're worried about the doneness of the pork, especially since this is a large roast, and stuffed at that, you can test the center of the roast with a meat thermometer. It should read 160 to 170 degrees F. before you prepare the roast for serving.

Even when fully cooked, I should perhaps note, the pork will be quite red at the outer edges. Once you've cut into the roast, you'll see a band of crimson around the chops where the smoke has penetrated most fully. This band has nothing to do with the doneness of the meat. Rather it marks the extra flavor contributed by the smoking.

About 30 minutes before you take the roast from the grill, baste it with the reserved mop for a finishing glaze. The crown will be magnificent — in appearance, aroma, and, most of all, taste. Oh, yes, and if you remember, do top the affair with those festive little paper frills nowadays often tucked in with a crown roast by the butcher.

HURRY-Q HONEY HAM

W hile it's true that barbecuing can't be hurried, here's a relatively quick dish for those times when unexpected company
descends or an equally unexpected impulse to sup on smoked
fare befalls you. The secret to readiness here lies in keeping a couple
of cooked ham steaks in the freezer. Come the guests or the chance
craving, simply zap the requisite number of steaks in the microwave
to defrost them, whip up a simple honey-mustard sauce to enhance
their flavor, and toss them into the smoker. They'll be ready in an
hour or less.

SERVES 4

2-pound fully cooked ham steak
½ cup honey
¼ cup prepared spicy mustard
2 tablespoons olive oil
chopped fresh parsley for garnish

Start a fire in the smoker, set out the ham steak, and pat it dry
with a paper towel.

In a small bowl, whip together the honey, mustard, and oil.

Once the coals have caught in the smoker's fire pan, add some
hardwood — wet apple and maple are traditional with ham — and
fill the water pan halfway with hot water. Place the ham steak on
the grill, brush liberally with some of the honey sauce, and put the
cover on the cooker.

Smoke the ham for 30 minutes at 200 to 220 degrees F., then turn
the steak, brush with honey sauce again, and smoke for 30 minutes
more.

In point of fact, you can get by with smoking the ham 15 minutes
to a side, since all you're really doing is heating it and letting the
spices and smoke permeate the meat. It will be more flavorsome,
though, given the extra smoking time.

Serve sprinkled with the parsley.

IN HOCK

P ork hocks, like pigs' feet and other extremities of this animal, are victuals you either can't abide or like hugely, usually because they were served often enough when you were growing up that you acquired a taste for them. Being in the latter camp myself, come summertime I often cook up a mess of jellied pigs' feet. Cold trotters in aspic are a particular delight on a hot day. I generally find myself eating them alone, though.

The same holds true for hocks. The fact is that the skin around a pork hock can be mighty chewy. Why this should bother anyone in a society in which billions of sticks of chewing gum are sold annually, I'm not certain. But there you are. The chewiness is what annoys most people.

So if you aren't a born-and-bred hock enthusiast, you have two options. You can either discard the tough outer rind before serving this dish, or you can go on to another recipe. If you do that, though, you'll be missing something special.

SERVES 3 TO 4

6 to 8 pork hocks, about 4½ to 6 pounds total
1 cup catsup
½ cup water
¼ cup lemon juice
3 tablespoons dark brown sugar
2 tablespoons cider vinegar
1 tablespoon paprika
½ teaspoon ground cloves

About 6 to 7 hours before you're going to muster the audacity to present this dish, place the hocks in a nonreactive dish or baking pan large enough for them to be laid out in a single layer.

In a small stainless steel or flameproof ceramic saucepan, combine the catsup, water, lemon juice, brown sugar, vinegar, paprika, and cloves. Whisk until well blended and smooth. Heat to a simmer and cook for 5 minutes, continuing to whisk.

Pour the marinade over the hocks, turn to coat well on both sides, and let steep while you fire up the smoker.

Once the coals are glowing, add wet wood and a pan of hot water. Reserving the marinade, place the pork hocks on the grill, flat side down.

Baste well with the reserved marinade, cover the cooker, and smoke the hocks at 210 to 230 degrees F. for 5 to 6 hours, or until they have long since reached an internal temperature of 160 to 170 degrees F., turning and basting the hocks after 1 hour and about every hour after that until they're done. While you have the smoker open to tend the hocks, check on the supplies of water and wet wood in their respective pans.

When smoked to perfection, the hocks will be black on the outside and oh-so-tasty on the inside.

CÔTE D'IVOIRE CARROT SALAD

The Ivory Coast hasn't suddenly become famous for its carrots as well as its cocoa. No, the name of this salad derives from the abode of the friends who first introduced us to it, the Izards, at the time living in Abidjan. Now the particular appeal the salad had for us may have been due to the fact that we'd just spent several months pushing a recalcitrant Peugeot through the largely trackless Sahara in order to reach that city and had in the process acquired a considerable craving for crisp fresh vegetables. All the same, our fondness for the dish has not since diminished.

Everyone who's tasted this simple salad agrees that it's nothing short of scrumptious. Like coleslaw, it goes particularly well with hearty smoked fare such as pork. Also like coleslaw, it improves with mellowing and is readily made up a day or two in advance of its serving, which saves preparation time on company occasions.

SERVES 4 TO 6

1 pound carrots, pared and coarsely grated
⅓ cup Dijon mustard
2 tablespoons white vinegar
⅓ cup olive oil

Place the carrots in a large mixing bowl and toss lightly with a fork to disperse any clumps.

Measure the mustard into a small bowl or cup, gradually mix in the vinegar, and then slowly add the olive oil, whisking all the while.

Pour the dressing over the carrots, toss well, and chill, tightly covered, in the refrigerator until needed.

6. HERE'S THE BEEF

As any fan of backyard grilling will tell you, it takes a tender cut to bring out the best of beef. Tough cuts turn tougher. Take brisket, for instance. Grilled brisket can present a more rubbery disposal problem than worn-out tires.

Now smoking, that's something different. Because of the low heat, long cooking time, and atmospheric moisture and fragrance surrounding the meat in the lidded cooker, smoking combines the tenderizing effects of braising or stewing with the extra flavor of wood smoke. The high fat content of brisket beef keeps it from drying out even during the extended smoking required to tenderize the cut, and by the time the meat is done, most of the fat has literally melted away.

From basic steak to Oriental flank steak, from an all-day roast to smokeburgers, and from short brisket to long, here's the beef, smoke-style.

"BURNT" BRISKET

The name of this dish comes from the fact that the meat looks burned after its prolonged cooking. The operative word here, however, is *looks*. The brisket isn't really burned, and it has none of the dry, bitter flavor associated with charred meat. Let's just say that it has a nice dark patina of smoke and spices.

When you buy brisket for smoking, think un-Sanforized. Brisket shrinks by as much as 30 to 40 percent when smoked. This is no drawback, since the reduction in mass concentrates the flavor of the meat.

A long brisket is essentially a packer-trimmed beef brisket, usually 8 to 12 pounds or more in weight, that's shipped whole for the local butcher to cut into smaller pieces. It has a thick layer of fat along one side in addition to that marbling the meat itself. So-called first-cut brisket, nearer the plate, is heavier than second-cut brisket, toward the shank. The closer the meat is to the shoulder, the more fibrous and laced with fat it is. If you're buying a whole brisket, you get it all, including the outer layer of fat, most of which will be dispersed during the smoking, seeping through the brisket and adding savor and tenderness to the meat.

Brisket is often seasoned first with a dry rub and then with a liquid mop. In this recipe, the rub and the mop ingredients are combined and applied together, starting out as what is arguably an uncommonly concentrated, syrupy marinade and then doubling as a basting sauce. There should be plenty of the spicy liquid left, even after it has served in both these capacities, from which to cobble up a dipping sauce for those for whom no dish can be too fiery.

SERVES UP TO 18

> 8- to 12-pound whole beef brisket
> 1 twelve-ounce can beer
> 1 cup corn oil
> ½ cup cider vinegar
> ¼ cup Worcestershire sauce
> ⅔ cup firmly packed dark brown sugar
> ½ cup paprika
> ¼ cup ground black pepper
> ¼ cup chili powder
> 2 teaspoons ground cumin

The day before this smoked brisket is to be on your menu, set out a large Ziploc-type plastic bag roomy enough for both the meat and the marinade. The sturdier version used for freezing, stronger than the ordinary storage variety, is definitely recommended here in view of the sticky, gooey sauce it is to contain.

Pour the beer, corn oil, vinegar, and Worcestershire sauce into the bag, close it, and swirl to mix. Add the brown sugar, paprika, pepper, chili powder, and cumin and swirl again, crushing between your fingers any lumps from the dry ingredients — the brown sugar is the most likely culprit — that settle undissolved to the bottom.

Put the brisket in the marinade, zip the bag shut, and work the liquid up around the meat to ensure that it's well saturated all around. Refrigerate overnight, turning once or twice if you think of it so the meat becomes more evenly permeated by the seasoning.

The following day, a good 12 hours before dinnertime, take the bagged brisket from the refrigerator and let it marinate at room temperature while you start the smoker and check that you have plenty of wood soaking. Maple, alder, or another mild wood would be a good choice here. This will be a long smoke, so there will be ample time for flavor and fragrance to enfold the meat.

Once the coals are glowing and you've added some wet wood, fill the water pan with hot water, drain the brisket briefly, reserving the marinade, and place it on the grill, fat side up.

Smoke the meat for 10 hours or longer at 200 to 220 degrees F. without turning and without peeking beneath the smoker lid except as necessary to check the cooker's coal, wood, and water supplies.

After its long smoke, baste the brisket with some of the reserved marinade, turn it over, and mop the other side. Smoke for another 30 minutes.

Shortly before you take the brisket from the grill, bring the remaining marinade-cum-mop to a simmer in a small stainless steel or flameproof ceramic saucepan and cook gently for 5 minutes. Serve the sauce as a dip.

SHIMMY-SHIMMY SHORT BRISKET

Most half briskets sold today are in the 4- to 5-pound range. Such a cut is small enough to make family fare for those not living cheaper by the dozen, and at the same time, it doesn't take all day to smoke. In cutting short briskets from long, however, butchers usually trim the edging layer of fat before putting the cuts out for sale. So if you want to take advantage of the fat rim's moisturizing and tenderizing propensities, you may have to order your brisket in advance. Ask the butcher to leave the fat layer on your half.

Because a brisket is smoked fat side up, the melting fat percolates through the meat, keeping it moist as it cooks. When the meat is fully smoked, the fat is gone, leaving behind only the juicy, succulent beef flavor.

SERVES 6 TO 8

4- to 5-pound half beef brisket
¼ cup firmly packed dark brown sugar
2 tablespoons chili powder
2 tablespoons ground cumin
2 tablespoons ground black pepper
1 tablespoon ground cayenne pepper
1 tablespoon ground celery seed

The day before you plan to serve the brisket, set it out on a platter large enough to give you some working room around it.

Measure the brown sugar, chili powder, cumin, black and cayenne peppers, and celery seed into a small mixing bowl and blend, working out any lumps with the back of the spoon. Pat the spices onto the brisket, pressing them in all around the meat. Refrigerate the seasoned brisket overnight in a sealed Ziploc-type plastic bag.

The following day, remove the meat from the refrigerator 7 to 8 hours before dinnertime to give it plenty of time to reach room temperature before smoking. Start a fire in your smoker some 3 hours later, build up a good bed of coals, add wet wood and a pan of hot water, and you'll be set.

Smoke the brisket, covered, at 200 to 220 degrees F. for 4 to 5 hours, or until fork tender, replenishing the wood and water pans as needed to ensure plentiful smoke.

This one will make your taste buds shimmy with delight.

ALL-DAY SMOKED BEEF

Roasts have always been long cookers, but for smoked roast beef, a whole day is not too long. In this particular recipe, the extra flavor of the meat is imparted not by a marinade but by the fragrance rising from the steaming liquid beneath it as it smokes.

For a tasty one-dish meal, add a few potatoes and onions to the water pan a couple of hours before dinnertime, some carrots about an hour later.

SERVES 6 TO 8

> 4- to 5-pound boneless beef roast
> olive oil
> 1 to 2 tablespoons garlic powder
> ground black pepper to taste
> 2 cups red wine
> 2 cloves garlic, peeled
> 2 bay leaves
> 2 teaspoons fresh rosemary
> 8 to 10 medium-size potatoes, peeled (optional)
> 8 to 10 small onions (optional)
> 4 large carrots, cut into 1-inch sections (optional)

Pat the roast dry, rub with olive oil, and sprinkle with the garlic powder and pepper. Set aside to rest while you start a fire in your smoker.

Since the roast will be cooking for the better part of the day, you'll want good, steady smoldering coals and plenty of wet wood beneath it. You'll also want to start out with a clean, foil-lined — since you'll actually be cooking in it — well-stocked water pan. Fill the pan almost two-thirds of the way up with hot water, then add the wine, garlic, bay leaves, and rosemary.

Smoke the roast, with the lid firmly on the cooker, at 200 to 220 degrees F. for 8 hours or more, checking the temperature occasionally and adding charcoal and soaked wood as needed. Make sure the level of the liquid in the water pan never drops to below one-third, and remember to use hot water when topping it off.

About 2 hours before you'll be ready to serve the roast, slip the potatoes and onions into the fragrantly simmering liquid in the water pan. Add the carrot sections 1 hour before dinnertime.

When you're ready to serve the roast, transfer it to a platter and fish the vegetables out of the water pan with a slotted spoon, letting them drain well before arranging them around the meat.

ORIENTAL FLANK STEAK

B ack in the sixties, when Susan and I were first married and living in New York on hope and high-octane postcollegiate drive, flank was about the cheapest cut going by the name of steak that you could buy. Known more for its sinewy toughness than anything else, it did have a lot of flavor nonetheless, and in the then-popular *Cookbook of the Seven Seas* by Dagmar Freuchen, wife of the famous explorer Peter Freuchen, Sue ran across a recipe that transformed this disdained cut of meat into a delicacy accorded rave reviews by our guests.

Peter Freuchen's explorations and sojourns in exotic lands, which once so captured the world's imagination, have vanished from the popular press. *Cookbook of the Seven Seas* lies somewhere in an unpacked box from one of our moves. And flank steak has become a luxury. But the recipe, modified over the years, as recipes are, and long since moved from the broiler category to the outdoor-cookery section of the kitchen card file, remains in the family, much esteemed.

SERVES 4 TO 6

2 beef flank steaks, 1¼ pounds each
½ cup sesame oil
⅓ cup sugar
¼ cup rice vinegar
¼ cup soy sauce
3 tablespoons minced fresh gingerroot
12 cloves garlic, peeled and put through a garlic press
6 medium-size scallions, greens included, chopped

The day before you plan to serve the flank steaks, lay them side by side in a shallow nonreactive ceramic or glass dish or on a serving platter large enough to accommodate them with their marinade.

Measure the sesame oil, sugar, vinegar, and soy sauce into a small mixing bowl and whisk until well blended. Stir in the ginger, garlic, and scallions.

Pour the marinade over the steaks, turn them to saturate both sides, and scoop some of the garlic and scallions up over them. Cover tightly with plastic wrap and marinate in the refrigerator overnight. Turn the steaks in the evening and again the following morning, scooping garlic and scallions over them each time.

About 2 to 2½ hours before dinnertime, start a fire in your smoker and build up a good bed of coals. Then add some wet wood, fill the water pan halfway with hot water, and transfer the steaks to the grill, reserving the marinade.

Cover the grill and smoke the steaks for 1½ to 2 hours at 210 to 230 degrees F.

Shortly before you're ready to serve the steaks, simmer the reserved marinade for 2 to 3 minutes. Place the smoked steaks on their serving platter and pour the hot marinade over them.

To serve, carve very thin slices from the steaks, keeping the knife nearly horizontal and working diagonally across the grain as if you were slicing a side of smoke-cured salmon. Between the long, slow cooking and your artful carving, the flank steak will melt in your mouth.

GARLICKED SKIRT STEAK

T he New York bar and restaurant where I moonlighted during my early writing career could have modeled for a college version of Cheers. At the Gold Rail, as this establishment was known, you could buy a large steak, an also large baked potato, salad, fresh crisp rolls, and the drink of your choice all for $1.19.

In part, the secret of the management's success lay in the second drink and the third and so on. To a great extent, however, it lay in the choosing of the meat. This was skirt steak, very toothsome, sometimes ever so slightly sinewy, cut from the plate, or belly, section of beef, and considered by most butchers to be trimmings fit only for grinding into hamburger. Today, when fajitas and other Tex-Mex dishes are much in vogue, skirt steaks sell for a premium, the site of the old Gold Rail is occupied by a Chinese restaurant, and the easy living of the sixties has been replaced by a mortgage.

All the same, skirt steaks are still a great buy, for they tend to be exceptionally flavorful. Personally, I'll take a good skirt steak over that symbol of luxury beef, a filet mignon, any day. Yes, filet mignon is tender, but if tenderness is the sole criterion of taste, then one might as well gum oatmeal, sans salt at that. However unrecognized or ignored the fact, filet mignon suffers from an extreme paucity of flavor. That's certainly not something anyone could say about a good garlicky skirt.

If you can't find skirt steak, sirloin tips, or flaps, may be substituted for it. They are often, in truth, just another label under which skirt is sold.

SERVES 2

> ¾- to 1-pound beef skirt steak
> 2 whole bulbs garlic, the cloves peeled and put through a garlic
>   press
> 1 teaspoon anchovy paste
> ¼ cup cider vinegar
> 3 tablespoons water
> 2 teaspoons Worcestershire sauce
> 4 tablespoons butter

The day before garlicked skirt is to be on your menu, set the steak out in a shallow nonreactive glass or ceramic dish.

To make the marinade for it, place the pressed garlic in a small mixing bowl and work the anchovy paste into it until the two are well blended. Add the vinegar, water, and Worcestershire sauce, stirring after each addition.

Pour the marinade over the steak, turn to saturate the meat on both sides, cover tightly with plastic wrap, and refrigerate overnight.

Fire up the smoker the next day about 2 hours before dinnertime. While a bed of coals is forming, drain the excess marinade from the steak into a small stainless steel or flameproof ceramic saucepan. Add the butter and heat just until the butter is melted, then remove from the stove.

Put some wet wood in your smoker's fire pan and hot water in the water pan, place the steak on the grill, baste with the marinade and butter mixture, and cover the cooker. Smoke the steak at 200 to 230 degrees F. for 1½ hours, turning it after the first 45 minutes and basting the other side.

ROLLED ROUND STEAK WITH MUSHROOMS AND PINE NUTS

A mushroom isn't just a mushroom anymore. The snowy white, rather bland supermarket standard-bearer now shares the bin with a whole range of once-esoteric relatives. The fresh shiitake is seen there quite regularly, as are the oyster and the crimini. Even the chanterelle makes a rare appearance among the others.

Such flavorsome fungi enhance many a dish, but it's the steak-and-mushroom combination that I find unbeatable. Here, pine nuts add marvelous textural contrast.

SERVES 4

1½- to 2-pound beef round steak
4 tablespoons butter
1 medium-size onion, thinly sliced
½ green bell pepper, finely chopped
2 cups coarsely chopped fresh shiitake mushrooms
½ cup pine nuts
1 egg, well beaten

About 3 to 3½ hours before dinnertime, start a fire in your smoker and get a good bed of coals going.

Lay the steak out on a cutting board or butcher block and trim off any excess fat. Then pound it well with a meat mallet, both to tenderize it and to stretch it flat. Try to get it as thin as possible without making holes in it.

To make the stuffing for the steak, melt the butter in a frying pan set over low heat, add the onion and pepper, and sauté until the onion slices are golden. Then add the mushrooms and cook just until they change color. You don't want to drive out all the liquid.

While the mushrooms are cooking, cut several lengths of untreated cotton cord and lay them out at 1-inch intervals on the cutting board or butcher block. Lay the steak lengthwise across the strings.

Remove the frying pan from the stove, add the pine nuts, quickly stir in the beaten egg, and pour the mixture onto the steak, keeping the filling toward the middle. Roll the steak, bring the cords up around it, and tie securely.

Add wet wood to your smoker's fire pan and hot water to the water pan, and put the steak on the grill and the lid on the cooker. Smoke the rolled round for 2½ to 3 hours at 210 to 230 degrees F.

A variation on this hardly ordinary stuffed steak is achieved by basting it with barbecue sauce as it cooks for a bit of added zing. Choose a baste from the sauce chapter in this book or use a favorite ready-made one, but whatever you do, don't use too much, or you'll overpower the lovely delicate flavor of the mushrooms.

PORTABELLA-STUFFED STEAK

As a child in Sweden, I knew where in the woods chanterelles could be found and by what moss-covered rocks the morels grew. Best of all, I knew of the secret fairy ring where the biggest boletuses would push through the forest soil year after year, and at the age of five I could be counted on to go out into the woods and return with a basketful for dinner.

Boletuses and morels are still not all that readily available here, but grand portabellas can often be found among the many mushroom varieties on produce shelves throughout the land. Of all the glorious fungi, these are my favorite, in part because their flavor most closely approximates that of the boletus.

Portabellas are great with steak. A thick cut stuffed extravagantly with these mushrooms and just a little sweet butter, then smoked lingeringly over a fragrant wood, is a bit of gustatory heaven. Involving no marinating, this dish is ideal for times when you haven't planned a day ahead.

SERVES 4

4 thick beef club steaks, about 4 to 5 pounds total
6 to 8 ounces portabella mushrooms, stemmed and thickly sliced
4 tablespoons chilled unsalted butter
coarsely ground black pepper to taste

About 2½ to 3½ hours before dinnertime, fire up your smoker and start a good bed of coals.

Cut a deep pocket in each steak from one side, taking care to leave the other three sides intact. Stuff each steak with as many of the sliced mushrooms as you can squeeze in without tearing the

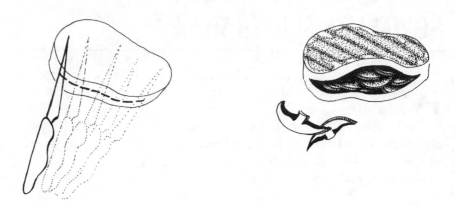

pocket. With a knife, slip thin pats of the butter into each pocket on both sides of the mushrooms.

Gently flatten each steak a bit to wedge the filling firmly in place, then sprinkle the outside with the pepper. Press the grains into the steak.

Smoke the steaks at 210 to 230 degrees F. for 1 to 1½ hours, then turn them and smoke for another 1 to 1½ hours. While you have the smoker open to turn the steaks, check the water and wood, replenishing them if necessary.

NETTLED STEAK

This unusual recipe came about because to my mind barbecue is country, country is horses, and horses mean nettles. Stinging nettles are not something you'll find in the produce department of your local supermarket — at least not yet. I suspect their introduction to those aisles is not far away, though. After all, nowadays we procure from those selfsame shelves fiddleheads, dandelion greens, mesclun salad, and a host of other provisions most people didn't dream of putting on their plates, much less in their mouths, a couple of decades ago. Yet the fact is that nettles, long popular in soups and vegetable dishes in northern Europe, are about as vitamin-packed a spring vegetable as you can find. And they grow rampant in our pasture.

So there I was in the kitchen one day pulling the tender leaves off some young nettles. In my youth, I'd picked the shoots bare-handed for the family table, but now I was wearing gloves, for unless you handle nettles exactly right, you'll quickly discover why the plants' common name includes the prefix *stinging*.

Into the kitchen walked our son, Revell. "Hey, you're cheating." Picking a plant up by its stem just so, he neatly pulled off the leaves, expertly avoiding the stinging hairs at their edges. Ah, the confidence of youth. I kept my gloves on.

With or without gloves, when one is picking nettles for culinary purposes, the thing to remember is that the plants must be young, preferably not over 6 inches tall. Older, larger nettles and those showing the hint of a flower forming make for a gritty sauce.

The flavor of nettles is mild and somewhat like that of spinach, although the green is rather more vibrant. Nettles are traditionally served with eggs, but any protein, including steak, turns them into a balanced meal.

SERVES 2

2 *thick beef strip steaks, about 1½ pounds total*
1 *cup concentrated beef stock or 2 beef bouillon cubes dissolved*
   in 1 cup boiling water
2 *tablespoons cider vinegar*
½ *teaspoon ground white pepper*
½ *teaspoon salt*
4 *cups firmly packed nettle leaves*
3 *tablespoons butter*
1 *teaspoon freshly ground cardamom seeds, white hulls*
   discarded

The day before you'll be smoking your nettled steaks, set out a reasonably deep nonreactive ceramic or glass dish in which they will fit snugly.

Pour the stock or bouillon into a fairly large stainless steel or flameproof ceramic saucepan and bring to a boil. Stir in the vinegar, white pepper, and salt. Add the nettle leaves, letting them wilt into the hot liquid, and simmer for 3 to 5 minutes, or until tender.

Cool the nettles slightly and scoop them into a blender or food processor. Add the butter and cardamom and puree until the mixture is smooth and creamy. It will be a surprisingly bright green.

Pour a little of the marinade into the deep dish you've set out. Press a steak into it and cover with more liquid, spooning the marinade down around the sides of the meat as well. Repeat for the other steak. Marinate the meat, covered tightly with plastic wrap and refrigerated, overnight.

Fire up your smoker a couple of hours before dinnertime. When it's hot, add some soaked wood, fill the water pan to the halfway mark with hot water, and place the steaks on the grill. Reserve the marinade.

Cover the cooker and smoke the meat at 200 to 230 degrees F. for 1 to 2 hours, the time depending on how rare or well-done you like your steak.

About 5 minutes before you're ready to transfer the steaks to their serving platter, heat the leftover marinade, letting it simmer briefly and gently. Pour it over the steaks before serving.

DOUBLE-MUSTARD STEAK

There's no way to hurry smoking. However, for those occasions when you suddenly crave a succulent smoked dish but are short on time, there are recipes that don't call for overnight marinating, speeding up your preparations to that extent, at any rate. The steak recipe given here is about as simple as any you'll find, yet the results are rich and enticing.

SERVES 2

2 thick boneless beef rib-eye steaks, about 1½ pounds total
your favorite prepared mustard, the tangier the better

Slather the steaks on both sides with a copious quantity of mustard and let rest at room temperature on a platter or a large piece of aluminum foil while you start the fire in your smoker.

Once the smoker is billowing, place the steaks on the grill over wet wood and a pan of hot water and cook at 200 to 230 degrees F., keeping the smoker covered, for about 45 minutes. Then turn the steaks and continue smoking for another 15 minutes, or until done to taste and quite irresistible any longer.

PEPPERED MUSTARD BUTTER

Mustard used in smoking meats adds only mild flavor, so it's not overdoing things to accent a mustard-spiced steak with this piquant mustard butter.

MAKES A LITTLE MORE THAN 1 CUP

1 cup (2 sticks) butter
2 tablespoons prepared mustard
freshly ground black pepper to taste
salt to taste (optional)

In a small bowl, let the butter reach room temperature, then cream until soft and smooth. Blend in the mustard. If you have used salted butter, simply add pepper to taste. If you're using sweet butter, and depending on the brininess of the mustard, you may want to add a dash of salt.

BRUSH AND TWIG STEAK

Yard work is an unending series of seasonal chores that have be-come part and parcel of twentieth-century ritual. Some tasks, like shoveling snow, are regional in nature — much talked about but little undertaken in the barbecue belt stretching across the southern United States. Other chores, such as gathering up storm-tumbled branches and other detritus descending from the trees, are universal, although the end results may vary. In our family, for in-stance, the final outcome of a yard cleanup is usually steak.

SERVES 1 — MULTIPLY BY THE NUMBER OF PERSONS TO BE SERVED

twelve-ounce beef sirloin or rib-eye steak
Worcestershire sauce to taste
freshly pressed garlic or garlic powder to taste
freshly ground black pepper to taste

Assuming that there are dead branches at hand, either on the ground or in a brush pile — out of sight behind the garage, perhaps, until you finally get rid of it someday — turn your attention to the steak first.

Place the meat on a cutting board or butcher block and, using a knife with a long blade, make crisscross slashes about ⅛ inch deep and ⅛ inch apart on both sides of the steak. Splash one side liberally with the Worcestershire sauce, sprinkle with the pressed garlic or gar-lic powder and the pepper, and slash again. Flip the steak and repeat on the other side. Let the steak rest while you start your cooking fire.

For this smoke, you won't need your water pan, so put it safely aside. Crumple a few sheets of newspaper and put them in the fire pan of your smoker. (There is, I feel, no truth to the rumor that the food section of the newspaper is the best for lighting barbecue fires.) Lay a lot of small twigs over the newspaper tepee fashion. Add first some finger-diameter branches, then half a dozen larger ones mea-suring an inch or so across. Don't worry if the tepee ends up higher than your smoker's grill. With the strike of a match or two, you'll burn it all down.

Light the fire. Once it's roaring, you may have to knock the wood down to lower the flames a bit. They should be leaping but barely licking the grill when you toss the steak on to cook.

Sear the steak for just a minute or two on each side. What you want is a nice set of black stripes from the grill, no charring.

As soon as both sides of the steak are zebracized, put the lid on your smoker to kill the flames. The vents of covered kettle barbecues such as the Weber need to be shut considerably to snuff out the flames, but not entirely, which would kill the glow of the coals as well.

Let the smoke billow — and billow it will — for 10 to 15 minutes, depending on the thickness of the steak and how rare or well-done you like it. As a rule of thumb, smoking a steak this way takes about twice as long as grilling it the traditional way. It also tastes twice as good, I think.

SMOKEBURGERS

Burgers, be they hamburgers or cheeseburgers, are the center-piece fare of summer cookouts — informal, even a little sloppy, conducive to relaxed talk and laughter. Ribs are great, but they keep you so busy licking fingers that the flow of conversation is curtailed. Steaks, well, I love a good steak, but steaks are knife-and-fork food, adding ever so slightly to the formality of an occasion. There are other simple cookout dishes. Sausages, from frankfurters to kielbasa, come to mind. The list could go on, certainly. Yet one dish after the other has a way of often being shunted from the summer cookout menu, leaving simplicity itself in the form of a really good hamburger.

Unfortunately, the ideal and reality often collide on the grill. Burgers cooked with flamethrower violence by hissing fat turn black and crisp on the outside but stay raw on the inside.

Now a hamburger in a smoker, on the other hand, sits serenely on the grill absorbing flavor for an hour or more, a sojourn that can transform even mediocre ground meat into something resembling sirloin. The pat of butter in the recipe, by the way, isn't necessary, even for the leanest grind. Burgers simply don't dry out when smoked. It's a seasoning trick I picked up from an old James Beard cookbook, and it's well worth the little extra fat for the subtle flavor it adds.

SERVES 1 — MULTIPLY BY THE NUMBER OF PERSONS TO BE SERVED

⅓ pound ground beef
2 teaspoons Worcestershire sauce
1 teaspoon garlic powder
1 teaspoon freshly ground black pepper
1 tablespoon chilled butter
1 English muffin
2 thick slices of your favorite cheese (optional)

About 1½ hours before your burger cookout, fire up your smoker and start a good bed of coals going. Then turn your attention to the hamburger preparation.

Place the meat in a mixing bowl large enough to accommodate the quantity you are preparing. If the hamburger comes from its packaging in a solid mass, break it apart lightly with a fork, lifting and separating rather than mashing it. Sprinkle the Worcestershire sauce, garlic powder, and pepper over the meat and toss to mix.

Shape a patty by squeezing gently, making every effort not to knead it. It's all right to let small pieces fall through your fingers. Your prime concern is not to mush the meat.

At the last minute, nudge the cold butter into the center of the burger and pat the meat back over it.

Add some wet wood or chips to the smoker's fire pan, fill the water pan halfway with hot water, and grease the grill lightly. Then put the meat on the grill and cover the cooker right away to keep all the swirling smoke inside.

A smokeburger should cook for roughly 1 hour at 200 to 220 degrees F. It need not be turned; it will take care of itself. All the same, I do turn mine after the first 30 minutes, just to give both sides those nice grill marks I associate with hamburgers.

I find that the hearty taste of an English muffin really goes better with a smokeburger than does the standard bland white bun. About 10 minutes before serving, I put one English muffin per burger, fork-split side down, on the grill to toast.

For a cheeseburger, top the meat patty with 2 slices of your favorite cheese — Swiss is an excellent foil for a smoked hamburger — about 10 to 15 minutes before taking it from the grill. If the cheese doesn't melt in that time, well, then just leave the burger on a little longer. It's gooey melted cheese or none at all in my book, and you can rest assured that as long as there's water in the water pan, there's really no way you can overcook smokeburgers.

MARVELOUS MARROW

The endless Old World controversy over the proper way to prepare marrowbones went the way of the marrowbones themselves a long time ago, together with the neighborhood butchers who supplied them — or so I always thought. Then, quite unexpectedly, this delicacy began appearing again — in the meat case of our local supermarket, of all places. A whole flood of memories came sweeping back when I first saw them there.

The two traditional ways of cooking and serving these long beef leg bones in former days were a matter as much of class as of culinary distinction. Cut into cross sections about 3 inches thick, the marrowbones were boiled wrapped in linen and then served upright, each one enfolded in a crisply ironed fresh damask napkin to spare diners' fingers both the heat of the bones and the oiliness of the insides. Alternatively, the bones were sawed into 3- to 4-inch lengths and the lengths were then split down the middle and baked. Either way, the marrowbones were presented complete with a narrow-bladed knife or a long marrow spoon expressly designed for scooping the marrow out onto warm toast.

For smoked marrow, either cut is fine. Seal the ends of the bone sections with a bit of flour paste to keep the delicate marrow in place as it cooks, then tuck the bones into the smoker along with whatever else you're cooking that day. Present the marrowbones within or without damask napkins as a mouthwatering preprandial delicacy.

SERVES 2 AS AN APPETIZER

> 4 marrowbones, about 3½ to 4 pounds total
> 1 tablespoon flour
> 2 teaspoons water
> triangles of hot toast

Assuming the smoker is already about its business for the day, your preparations for this dish are quite simple.

Lay the bones out on a handy work surface, cut side up in the case of the long variety. If what you've bought is cross sections — well, take your pick of ends to put facing up.

Measure the flour into a small bowl or cup, add a little of the water, and stir until smooth. Add more water until you have a paste thick enough to hold together, thin enough to spread.

Apply a thin layer of the flour paste over the very ends of the bones. You don't want to cover the trench of marrow along the top of the long bones. In the case of the round ones, cover the ends you can see, give the paste a few minutes to set a bit, and then turn the bones over and seal the other end of each.

Smoke the marrowbones for 1 to 2 hours at 210 to 230 degrees F. A little less or a little more heat is perfectly acceptable if what you're cooking next to them is smoking at a different temperature.

Serve the bones as they come from the smoker, golden and juicy, with thin triangles of hot toast to spread the marrow on. A slender knife or a demitasse spoon will answer for scooping out the rich, buttery marrow.

JERKY

S moked beef jerky, once a staple of wilderness canoe trips and mountain treks, has invaded supermarkets and convenience stores, where the gathered habitués nibble the chewy meat on the way to their parked cars. This modern plastic-wrapped jerky is a product fashioned from ground meat suffused with flavoring whose origin is reputed to lie somewhere in the machinery used to manufacture dog treats. While the story is no doubt apocryphal, I mention it here by way of warning that the commercial jerky now so prevalent bears little resemblance to the down-home version.

Jerky is different from most barbecue fare in that it is smoked dry. Leave the water out of the water pan when cooking this one. I do recommend leaving the pan of a silo cooker in place, however, both to catch any drippings from the meat and to ensure that the direct heat of the fire is deflected away from the drying beef, which needs to cure slowly. Line the pan with aluminum foil to keep the drippings from scorching the bottom and to save on cleanup time. In the case of covered kettle grills like the Weber, just make sure the fire is well off to one side and the meat to the other so it's dried by indirect heat.

Sugar and salt, together or separately, have been used as preservatives for eons, although only lately have researchers discovered why they work in that capacity. In and of themselves, neither salt nor sugar possesses biocidal properties. However, at concentrated levels, they both serve as moisture traps, binding so effectively to any available liquid that they produce in their surroundings something called — in what must surely be a classic case of understatement — a low water activity area. In short, there's simply not enough moisture left in their vicinity to permit the growth of bacteria, fungi, or yeasts. In a sense, then, sugar and salt desiccate these organisms to death.

The actual application of the sugar and salt is a very subjective process. It's possible to smoke jerky without using a rub of sugar and salt at all, provided the moisture is driven entirely out of it by prolonged smoking. It's equally possible to coat the meat with so much sugar and salt that it's almost frosted. Only you can decide what will suit your taste. At its most seasoned extreme, though, a surface layer of salt and sugar will actually draw atmospheric humidity to itself so that beads of moisture form on the meat. At this stage, you've definitely gone too far.

Since the actual amount of sugar or salt absorbed by your particular batch of jerky is generally an unknown variable, it's a good idea to refrigerate the strips, tightly wrapped, for long-term storage, say more than a few days.

BASIC JERKY

A bicycle snack much favored by our children, jerky has its practical uses on long tours. Exceptionally light in weight, tightly packed with both protein and flavor, and high in the salt so easily depleted on hot summer days when one is struggling up hills sped down but a few hours earlier, jerky easily pays its way in the fanny pack. What more does the cyclist need but the clamp-on water bottle?

> 1½ pounds beef flank steak
> ½ cup sugar
> ½ cup noniodized salt

You'll need to allow about 4 to 6 hours for making a batch of jerky, and the first step will be to start a fire in your smoker and settle the coals in. You want steady but very low heat for this one.

Pat the steak dry with a paper towel and cut it across the grain into slices ¼ to ⅜ inch thick. Hold the knife so that the blade makes an angle 30 degrees or less to the horizontal, giving you broad but thin slices.

Blend the sugar and salt together and rub the mixture into the meat to taste.

Smoke the flank strips for 3 to 5 hours at 130 to 180 degrees F. If you have trouble keeping the heat in your smoker at that low a temperature, prop the lid open just a bit with a stick until the temperature drops to the desired range. Use plenty of wet wood, but remember to smoke dry. Do not — *repeat, do not* — add water to the water pan.

When the strips are dry enough to break when bent double, remove them from the grill and allow them to cool. Package individually in plastic wrap.

Refrigerate the jerky for storage longer than a few days.

SPICY JERKY

For a spicier jerky than the plain-Jane sugared-and-salted variety, use your imagination and personal taste. The following is a suggestion.

1½ pounds beef flank steak
¼ cup sugar
¼ cup noniodized salt
2 teaspoons paprika
2 teaspoons garlic powder
2 teaspoons ground black pepper
1 teaspoon ground ginger

Fire up your smoker and start settling the coals in for a long, slow smoke before starting the rub.

Pat the meat dry with a paper towel and slice it, with the blade of the knife 30 degrees to the horizontal, across the grain, creating strips ¼ to ⅜ inch thick.

In a small mixing bowl, blend together the sugar, salt, paprika, garlic powder, pepper, and ginger. Rub this mixture into the meat.

Add plenty of soaked wood to your cooker's fire pan before putting the spiced strips on the grill, but don't fill the water pan. Give the jerky 3 to 5 hours of smoke at 130 to 180 degrees F., propping the lid open a crack if the temperature threatens to rise disastrously beyond the desired range.

When the strips are chewy-crisp, remove them from the heat, let cool, and store individually in plastic wrap. Refrigerate to store longer than a few days.

JERKED JERKY

You might have guessed that I wouldn't be able to resist including a jerky recipe with a name like this. The Jamaican version is made in basically the same way as any other except that here, once the meat has been coated in spices, it's allowed to age, wrapped tightly and refrigerated at least overnight, before it's smoked.

1½ *pounds beef flank steak*
¼ *cup molasses*
¼ *cup cider vinegar*
¼ *cup noniodized salt*
1 *tablespoon ground black pepper*
1 *teaspoon crushed red pepper*
1 *teaspoon ground cinnamon*
½ *teaspoon ground nutmeg*
½ *teaspoon ground ginger*

The day before the one to be devoted to replenishing the jerky jar, slice the flank steak across the grain into broad but thin strips ¼ to ⅜ inch thick, holding the knife so that the blade makes an angle 30 degrees or less to the horizontal. Set the meat aside while you put together the seasoning mix for the jerky.

Pour the molasses and vinegar into a medium-size mixing bowl and add the salt, black and red peppers, cinnamon, nutmeg, and ginger. Whisk until well blended and free of lumps.

Transfer the spice mixture to a Ziploc-type plastic bag, add the flank strips, seal the bag, and swish the pieces around in the seasoning until they are well coated. Refrigerate overnight.

Start a fire in your smoker about 30 minutes before you'll be putting the flank strips on to smoke. You'll need a good bed of coals for the jerky, one that will provide long, steady heat but not too much of it.

Add plenty of soaked wood to your cooker's fire pan, but remember to leave the water pan empty. Before putting the meat on the grill, gently pat the pieces dry with a paper towel to remove excess moisture.

Smoke the jerky for 3 to 5 hours at 130 to 180 degrees F., propping the cooker lid open a crack if the temperature rises much higher than that.

When the strips are done enough to break when bent double, let cool, then wrap individually in plastic. To keep for longer than a few days, refrigerate.

7. SOMETHING SPECIAL: LAMB, VENISON, BUFFALO

The foods people favor are often discernibly regional. In New England, for instance, a recurrent feature in autumn fare is corned beef and cabbage — but try to find that dish on a menu in Alabama.

Then too, what's considered choice varies with the times. At the turn of the century, chicken was an infrequent entrée. On those rare occasions when the bird did find its way to the table, it was in soups, stews, or pot pies, a hen at the end of its laying years being too skinny and tough for any other presentation. Nowadays chicken, much transformed, is a preferred meat, touted not only for its low price but also for its tenderness, tastiness, and reduced fat.

For another example, lobster was in Pilgrim times a meal of last resort, consumed by those too poor to dine on anything else. Today the big crustacean is highly prized. Meanwhile mutton, long a staple in much of Europe, lost its preeminence to beef, while in the States, the once-common buffalo vanished almost altogether in the late 1800s, along with the empty plains it roamed unhindered by harrow or scythe.

Such shifts in time and taste remove certain dishes from the unremarkable to the ennobled. Among these newly special treats, lamb, venison, and buffalo rank high.

Of the three, lamb is the most easily procurable, found fresh in increasing variety at the supermarket meat counters that never entirely abandoned it, at least in its imported frozen form. However, specialty shops stocking game are becoming more and more prevalent, widening this market once confined to informal exchanges among hunters and their acquaintances, while ranch-raised buffalo is now shipped to all parts of the country by purveyors of this progressively more popular meat.

STUFFED LEG OF LAMB

I n this delightful dish, the silky spinach, creamy cheese, and crunchy pine nuts contrast luxuriously with the succulent, rich texture of the lamb.

Have the leg of lamb boned and trimmed for you, making sure you mention that you'll be stuffing it. I've purchased cryovac-packed boned leg of lamb in the supermarket, and while the flavor is passable, the crude boning more often than not involves removing the skeletal structure, with no thought to achieving an attractive dressed roast.

SERVES 6 TO 8

> 3- to 4-pound boneless leg of lamb
> 2 cloves garlic, peeled and bruised
> olive oil

THE STUFFING
> ¾ pound fresh spinach, stems removed
> ½ cup pine nuts
> 2 cups grated fontina cheese

THE SAUCE
> ¼ cup olive oil
> 3 cloves garlic, peeled and slivered
> 1 large leek, dark green top removed, chopped
> 2 large bay leaves
> ½ teaspoon crushed red pepper
> ½ cup white wine
> ¼ cup balsamic vinegar
> 1 tablespoon sugar
> 10 fresh basil leaves, minced

Light a fire in your smoker 4 to 5 hours before you want to serve this dish, adding plenty of coals to establish a good bed.

Lay out several lengths of untreated cotton cord long enough to later be tied around the leg of lamb, placing the strings about 1 to 1½ inches apart.

Open out the leg of lamb and rub both sides well with the garlic, then brush the meat all over with olive oil. Position the lamb lengthwise on the cotton cords so that once it's stuffed, it can be rolled and tied back into a leg-of-lamb shape.

Put a large nonreactive pot of water to boil on the stove, and when it's bubbling, add the spinach. Bring the water just back to a boil, then remove from the burner and drain the greens immediately.

Toast the pine nuts in a frying pan set over low heat, shaking the pan gently until the nuts are lightly browned.

Spread the spinach evenly over the lamb, leaving room at the edges so the greens won't be pressed out when the meat is rolled. Sprinkle the cheese over the spinach, then sprinkle the pine nuts over the cheese.

Roll the roast, tucking in the ends if need be, and tie securely.

Add some wet wood and perhaps a few fresh rosemary branches to your smoker's fire pan and fill the water pan at least halfway with hot water. Place the stuffed lamb on the grill, cover the cooker, and smoke at 210 to 230 degrees F. for 3 to 4 hours, the time depending primarily on how well-done you like your lamb.

About 1 hour before you plan to serve the lamb, heat the olive oil for the sauce in a medium-size nonreactive pan and sauté the garlic over low heat until golden. Add the leek, bay leaves, and crushed red pepper, and continue to sauté, stirring occasionally, until the leek bits are soft.

Pour in the wine and vinegar and sprinkle on the sugar, bring to the boiling point, then lower the heat and simmer the sauce gently for 10 to 12 minutes, stirring occasionally.

Remove and discard the bay leaves. Then pour the mixture — carefully, since it will be hot — into a blender or a food processor. Puree until smooth. Return the creamed sauce to the pan and keep warm until ready to serve.

When the lamb is done to your liking, transfer it from the grill to its platter or board and let rest a few minutes for easier carving. Meanwhile, stir all but a bit of the basil into the sauce, pour it into a sauceboat, and garnish with a sprinkle of the reserved herb leaves.

SMOKED RACK OF LAMB WITH DILL SAUCE

D ill is found abundantly in northern European dishes, associated with fish and pickles but also with lamb. The delicate flavor of the fresh herb best complements smoked lamb, however, where it's reserved for accompaniment rather than being used in the cooking itself.

If the quantity of garlic called for in the recipe seems excessive, bear in mind that much of this bulb's initially pungent flavor is converted to a mild sweetness during prolonged smoking.

SERVES 3 TO 4

2- to 3-pound rib rack of lamb, frenched for easier carving
10 cloves garlic, peeled and slivered
olive oil
fresh spinach leaves for garnish (optional)

Start building up the coals in your smoker about 3½ to 4½ hours before you plan to serve the rack of lamb. Then turn your attention to the meat.

With a sharp paring knife, make small slits about 1 inch apart between all the ribs and insert a sliver of garlic in each slit. Then gently brush the rack with olive oil, being careful not to dislodge the garlic slivers.

Place some wet wood in your smoker's fire pan — a branch or two of fresh sage as well will add heavenly flavor — and fill the water pan halfway with hot water. Then put the rack on the grill and smoke at 210 to 230 degrees F. for 3 to 4 hours, or until very tender and succulent but never overdone.

This rack of lamb is spectacular presented on a bed of rinsed and

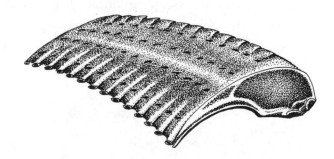

crisped spinach leaves, and a dill sauce is a particularly appealing addition when the lamb is served with steamed or roasted new red potatoes and just-barely-cooked fresh garden peas.

DILL SAUCE

Creamy and white, this sauce redolent of fresh dill is the perfect foil for a crusty, smoky-flavored rack of lamb. I like my dill sauce very dilly, but you're welcome to reduce the amount of that herb in the recipe if you like a subtler version.

MAKES A LITTLE MORE THAN 1½ CUPS

>   3 tablespoons butter
>   2 tablespoons flour
>   1½ cups milk
>   ½ cup minced fresh dill, stems removed
>   ¼ teaspoon ground white pepper
>   ¼ teaspoon salt

Melt the butter in a small saucepan set over low heat. Add the flour a little at a time, stirring to a smooth paste after each addition. Don't let the roux brown; you want a white sauce.

Slowly blend in the milk and heat, whisking constantly, until the sauce thickens. Stir in the dill, reserving a scant spoonful for garnish, and add the white pepper and salt. Blend until smooth and transfer to a warmed sauceboat to serve, garnished with the reserved spoonful of dill.

LAMB CHOPS WITH *RECAITO CRIOLLO*

M int jelly is such a traditional accompaniment to lamb that one almost expects a touch of shimmering green whenever this meat is served. Here the color accent is provided by the more subtle verdancy of the Puerto Rican condiment *recaito criollo*, prepared from cilantro, peppers, onions, garlic, and oregano. This "green catsup" is found in the Latin American section of most supermarkets.

SERVES 3 TO 4

> *4 to 6 thick lamb rib chops, about ⅓ pound each*
> *8 to 12 tablespoons prepared* recaito criollo

About 2 to 2½ hours before you want to serve these lamb chops, lay them out on a platter and spread over the top of each a scant tablespoonful of the *recaito criollo*. Turn the chops and spread the other side with an equal amount of the sauce. Then let the chops rest while you fire up your smoker.

Once the coals are glowing in your smoker's fire pan, add some wet wood, fill the water pan halfway with hot water, and smoke the chops, tightly covered by the cooker's lid, at 200 to 220 degrees F. for 1½ to 2 hours, perhaps a little less if you like your lamb rosy.

These chops will delight anyone fond of cilantro.

LAMB CHOPS WITH GREEN PEPPERCORNS

G reen peppercorns, primarily French and Spanish by association, were a culinary find of the eighties in the States. No
longer a novelty possessing the mystique of the newly in vogue,
they still go very well with lamb, superbly so with smoked lamb.

SERVES 3 TO 4

> 4 to 6 thick lamb rib chops, about ⅓ pound each
> 3 to 4 tablespoons pickled green peppercorns
> 1 tablespoon ground black pepper
> 1 tablespoon paprika
> 1 teaspoon ground cloves

Start a fire in your smoker about 2 to 2½ hours before your
planned dinnertime. Then turn your attention to the lamb.

Cut a fairly long, deep slit in each chop on the side opposite the
bone, as if for stuffing. Coax a couple of teaspoonfuls of the green
peppercorns into each pocket and pat the chops closed to help
spread the peppercorns out inside.

In a small bowl or cup, stir together the black pepper, paprika,
and cloves. Dust both sides of each chop with the seasoning.

Add some wet smoking wood to your cooker's fire pan and hot
water to the water pan, then place the chops on the grill. Smoke,
covered, at 200 to 220 degrees F. for 1½ to 2 hours. If you like your
lamb on the pink side, check the chops a little earlier than that.

The peppercorns wrapped in the tender lamb will still be crisp
when the chops are served, adding delightful textural contrast.

VENISON STEAK WITH JUNIPER BERRIES

Venison is autumn fare, and autumn is when the sumac and juniper berries abound. No wonder they're immutably associated with game.

Sumac, traditional in Middle Eastern cooking, lends a lovely flavor to venison. However, in our part of the woods, one must know the good sumac from the bad, so we usually leave this spice off the menu unless Shokoofeh or another of our Mideastern friends is with us to do the picking.

There's no mistaking juniper berries, though, and besides their presence in the wild, they're now available dried on most supermarket spice shelves. When it comes to cooking with these berries, the trick is to use enough of them.

SERVES 4

>
> 4 venison steaks, ½ to ¾ pound each
> ½ cup gin
> 12 juniper berries, fresh or dried
> ¼ cup red wine vinegar
> 1 tablespoon sugar
> ¼ cup olive oil

The night before you plan to serve these steaks, lay them out in a nonreactive dish or pan large enough to accommodate them with a marinade.

Pour the gin into a small stainless steel or flameproof ceramic saucepan. Crush the juniper berries with a mortar and pestle and add them to the juniper-flavored alcohol. Heat briefly, then light the alcohol and let it burn until the volume of liquid has been reduced by about one-half. Blow out the flame and add the vinegar and sugar, stirring to mix well.

Pour the marinade over the steaks, turning them to saturate both sides. Cover and refrigerate the venison in its marinade overnight.

The following day, about 2½ to 3½ hours before you want the venison to be ready, start a fire in your smoker. While the coals are heating, transfer the steaks from their marinade to a platter, reserving the liquid in which they were steeping.

Brush the steaks with the olive oil, sealing in the moisture from the marinade.

Add wet wood to your smoker's fire pan and hot water to the water pan, then place the steaks on the grill. Smoke them, covered, at 200 to 220 degrees F. for 2 to 3 hours, turning and basting them with the reserved marinade every 45 minutes or so until they're well-done.

Serve the venison steaks with buttery mashed sweet potatoes and a hearty fall vegetable like brussels sprouts — steamed just to tenderness and still prettily green.

VENISON CHOPS WITH WASABI SAUCE

The gamy taste often associated with venison is far stronger in repute, gained primarily by unfamiliarity with the meat, than in actuality. This is not to say that venison doesn't have a flavor clearly its own.

The curious thing about taste is that one's nose often plays as much a part in sensing its nuances as one's palate does. A notable example of this phenomenon is the savoring of horseradish. In this dish, the nose-tingling pungency of that root and the distinctive savor of venison are a perfect match.

Freshly grated horseradish can be used here, but because it's a condiment not habitually in residence in most refrigerators, the recipe instead lists wasabi, the green-tinted horseradish powder now found in the Oriental section of most supermarkets, which keeps almost indefinitely without refrigeration yet doesn't lose its snap.

A wonderful accompaniment to smoked venison is roasted chestnuts, another fall phenomenon. So while you're waiting for these chops to reach perfection, toss some chestnuts on the grill — a liberal supply of them, for in spite of your best efforts, they may still be all nibbled up before the meal. Don't forget, though, to slit the tip of each chestnut before putting it in the smoker to let the steam escape. Otherwise the nuts will explode just like popcorn.

SERVES 4

4 to 6 venison chops, ⅓ to ½ pound each
¼ cup olive oil

THE SAUCE
3 teaspoons wasabi
3 teaspoons water
3 tablespoons butter
2 tablespoons flour
1½ cups milk

About 2½ to 3½ hours before dinnertime, fire up your smoker and establish a good bed of coals. As soon as they're glowing, add some heavy smoking wood such as oak and set the water pan, filled halfway with hot water, in place.

Brush the venison chops with the olive oil, place them on the grill, and smoke them, tightly covered with the cooker lid, at 200 to 220 degrees F. for 2 to 3 hours, or until well-done.

When the chops are nearly ready, start the sauce for them. In a small cup or bowl, mix the wasabi and the water to a smooth paste. Set aside.

Melt the butter in a small saucepan. Stir the flour into the butter a little at a time, and once the mixture is well blended, begin adding the milk, again a little at a time. Heat until lightly thickened, add the wasabi paste, whisk until smooth, and pour into a warmed sauceboat to serve with the chops.

BUFFALO ROAST

B uffalo lends itself naturally not only to the smoky flavor of barbecuing but to the slowness of this culinary technique as well. Because the meat is very lean, it readily dries out when subjected to conventional cooking, whereas the low heat and circulating moisture of a smoker help it to retain its succulence and flavor.

SERVES 4 TO 6

3- to 4-pound buffalo roast
2 strips bacon, cut into ½-inch pieces
2 cups strong black coffee
1 cup white vinegar
3 tablespoons dark brown sugar
6 garlic cloves, peeled and put through a garlic press
6 medium-size onions, thinly sliced
6 whole cloves
3 tablespoons butter
2 tablespoons flour
pepper to taste
salt to taste

Two days before roast bison is to be on your menu, set out a deep nonreactive pan or bowl or a Ziploc-type bag into which the roast will fit together with the marinade.

Using a small, sharp paring knife, make small slits about 1 inch apart all around the roast and wedge a piece of the bacon into each one. Place the roast in its marinating pan or bag and set aside.

To make the marinade, pour the coffee into a medium-size pitcher or bowl, add the vinegar, sugar, and garlic, and mix well.

Pour the marinade over the roast, turn the meat in the pan or bag to help the liquid penetrate all sides, seal, and refrigerate. Turn the roast in its marinade once or twice a day until you're ready to cook it.

On the day you plan to serve the roast, start a fire in your smoker about 7½ to 8½ hours before dinnertime. Check that you have plenty of wood soaking, for this will be a long smoke.

While the coals are heating, set out a piece of heavy-duty aluminum foil large enough to enclose the roast and then some. Lay the onion slices in the center of the foil to form a base for the meat. Scatter the cloves over the onions. Take the roast from its marinade, reserving the extra liquid, and place the meat on top of the bed of onions and cloves. Bring the foil up around the meat, pressing it gently to form a snug package, and fold it over the top of the roast.

Add some wet wood to your smoker's fire pan and hot water to the water pan. Then transfer the wrapped roast to the grill, being careful not to puncture the foil. Open the package just a crack at the top to let smoke in without allowing too much of the moisture from the onions to escape.

Cover the cooker and smoke the buffalo at 200 to 220 degrees F. for 6 to 7 hours, or until tender and succulent, replenishing the supplies of wet wood and hot water as needed. Then prepare to give it a final moisturizing with the reserved marinade.

About an hour before serving, bring the reserved marinade to a boil in a medium-size saucepan. Gently widen the opening at the top of the roast's foil pack and pour the marinade slowly over the meat. Let the buffalo steam in its wrapping for 1 hour more, making sure your soaked wood is yielding plenty of smoke.

When you take the roast from its foil pack, pour the remaining marinade and onions left at the bottom — carefully, as they will be steaming hot — into a blender or food processor. Puree to a smooth gravy base.

Melt the butter in a small saucepan set over low heat. Stirring constantly, add the flour a little at a time, blending until you have a satiny roux. Then pour some of the pureed stock into the pan and heat, whisking steadily, until creamy. Mix in more stock until the gravy is as thick as you like it. Add pepper and salt to taste and serve.

PEMMICAN

The chuck wagon played a large part in our childhood games of cowboys and Indians, baked beans being the lunch of choice during those days. Over the years, my taste for the legumes diminished, along with the popularity of the game, no longer politically correct for children to play. What does remain, for me, is a fondness for pemmican, or at least the idea of pemmican, that wilderness survival staple so central to roaming the range in the imagination of every child I knew.

Buffalo was the primary ingredient of pemmican, and now that the meat is once more available, you might want to try making a batch of this venerable progenitor of sports food. Lean, mean, and tasty, it's a high-energy pick-me-up for bike trips and hikes.

>   *1 pound buffalo meat*
>   *½ cup raisins*
>   *2 tablespoons lard*
>   *2 tablespoons suet*
>   *1 teaspoon lemon juice*

Mixing up the pemmican will take about 30 minutes or so after the meat is dried, so start a fire in your smoker about 4½ to 5½ hours before you want to turn your attention to the task.

Start building up a good bed of coals for a long, slow smoke. While the coals are heating, slice the buffalo meat across the grain into thin strips no more than ¼ inch thick.

Add some wet wood to your smoker's fire pan, but don't put any water in the water pan, as the meat should be smoked dry. If what you have is a silo smoker, leave the pan in place, both to catch any drippings and to keep the heat circulating indirectly. Line the pan with aluminum foil, though, to prevent scorching and to save on cleanup time. If you're smoking the meat in a kettle smoker, you need only make sure you place the meat to one side, away from the fire.

Lay the buffalo strips out on the grill, well separated, and smoke them, tightly covered by the lid of the cooker, at 160 to 180 degrees F. for 4 to 5 hours, or until the pieces are dry enough to snap when bent.

When the strips are thoroughly dried, remove them from the grill and let cool. Then either put them through a meat grinder or chop them finely with a knife. Next, pound the ground meat into a powder with a wooden pestle in a wooden bowl. Alternatively, the meat can be pulverized in a blender or food processor set on its slowest speed. You may have to process small portions of the meat at a time to achieve a fine, even powder.

Transfer the powdered meat to a mixing bowl and place the raisins in the mortar or the blender or food processor, as the case may be. Grind the raisins thoroughly as well, then mix them in with the meat.

In a small saucepan set over low heat, melt the lard and the suet together. When they are well liquefied, stir in the lemon juice.

Pour the liquid mixture over the meat and raisins and blend well. Fingers do the best job of this. Once the mix has begun to adhere, pinch off pieces of it and shape them into patties ½ inch thick and 1 to 3 inches in diameter, the size depending mostly on how well the particular batch of pemmican "dough" you're working with holds together.

The pemmican patties can be packaged individually in plastic wrap. Pemmican needs no refrigeration unless it's to be kept for months on end.

8. WINGS AND THINGS

Chicken, turkey, and other fowl lend themselves splendidly to smoke cooking. No other means of preparing them produces dishes quite so juicy, succulent, and tender. The one drawback for some people is that when you smoke a whole bird, you don't get crispy skin. Then again, today's cholesterol-conscious diners tend to eschew this portion of the fowl anyway. Believe me, once you've had fresh smoked turkey, you'll wonder what that dry thing you used to eat for Thanksgiving really was.

CHICKEN ON A THRONE

This dish is a classic case of macho southern good-old-boy fooling around that ended up being a grand success. In fact, it's one of the tastiest poultry platters you'll ever serve.

The original trick was to remove the top of a can of beer with a can opener, drink half the beer, insert the can — keeping it upright, of course — into the cavity of a chicken where the stuffing usually goes, and then balance the bird and the beer can on the grill, propping the chicken legs forward on the rack to help steady it. Now if a number of chickens were involved, and if they kept falling over, necessitating the opening of yet more beer cans — well, you get the picture. Still, there's no denying that chicken cooked in this particular manner was about as moist and tender as it could be.

Over the years, the beer-can ploy was refined by the addition of spices and other flavorings to the beer, making for an even more succulent bird. However, one questionable feature continued to taint the technique. Beer cans are imprinted with colored inks, and these colored inks contain heavy metals less than healthy for your digestive system.

No one knows for sure that ingesting chicken cooked on a beer can is going to destroy your nervous system. But why take a chance? There are enough other excellent chicken recipes around and enough other ways to poison ourselves in the modern world without indulging in this one.

However, the picture has changed with the advent of Willie's Chicken Sitter. Impersonating a beer can with a preposterously flared and flattened bottom, the Chicken Sitter is a heatproof ceramic contraption modeled after those untippable coffee mugs used on shipboard, sans handle. It does everything the beer can does and more. Okay, so it doesn't supply the beer, but you'd have to buy that anyhow.

SERVES 4

3- to 4-pound fryer

THE RUB
2 teaspoons onion powder
1 teaspoon white pepper
½ teaspoon ground sage
½ teaspoon ground thyme
½ teaspoon dried rosemary, crushed
½ teaspoon salt

THE SITTER SOP
¾ cup beer
½ cup white vinegar
¼ cup water
¼ lemon
1 teaspoon black peppercorns
½ teaspoon ground sage

The night before you plan to serve this dish, rinse the chicken briefly under running water, drain, and pat dry inside and out with paper towels. Let rest while you prepare the rub.

In a Ziploc-type plastic bag large enough to hold the chicken, mix together the onion powder, white pepper, sage, thyme, rosemary, and salt. Add the chicken, seal the bag, and shake well to ensure that the bird is well dusted all over. Refrigerate the spiced fowl overnight.

About 3 to 3½ hours or so before dinnertime, remove the chicken from the refrigerator and let it rest at room temperature while you start a fire in your smoker. Then, when the coals are glowing, turn your attention back to the bird.

Pour the beer into the Chicken Sitter and add the vinegar and water. Then squeeze the lemon juice right into the Sitter and drop the peel in after it, followed by the peppercorns. Shake the sage in and swirl the Sitter gently to blend the mixture inside it.

Set the chicken on the Sitter by wedging the bottom cavity of the bird over the rim and down as far as it will go. In the case of a small bird, you may have to enlarge the cavity with a couple of short slits before the chicken will slide easily over the neck of the Sitter.

Add some wet wood to your smoker's fire pan and place the Sitter-sitting chicken on the grill with the bird's legs extended to complete a stabilizing tripod.

Close the cooker and smoke the chicken for 2½ to 3 hours at 200 to 230 degrees F. The liquid in the Chicken Sitter will not need to be replenished. However, don't forget to fill the water pan beneath it with hot water as well for an all-around moist and tender bird.

JAMAICAN JERKED CHICKEN BREASTS

n the hot and spicy category, Jamaican jerked dishes have a long and enviable history of popularity on their native island. Only recently, however, has this fiery cinnamon-accented fare gained similar favor abroad.

The traditional cinnamon and allspice seasoning of Jamaican jerk, often with considerable understatement described as "assertive," originally complemented meat preserved by sun drying on that tropical Caribbean isle, the spices serving to mask the odor and taste of victuals gone by much as they accomplished the same objective in Europe during the Middle Ages. Today jerk seasoning is used purely for flavoring, and only the pleasant smells remain.

The tamarind concentrate listed in the recipe is available in Asian markets, often in the form of the soup base *canh chua me,* which is enhanced with a bit of onion, shrimp powder, and other complementary flavorings. Another form in which it's found is the Thai *keo me,* or candied tamarind, spiced with sugar, salt, and hot chili pepper. *Keo me* is a surprisingly good candy — our kids love it — but if you use it in cooking, make sure you cut the pieces in half, for quite often they contain a seed. Habanero chilies are now found at most supermarkets.

The established way to mix jerk seasoning is by slowly pounding the spices to a powder with a mortar and pestle. Although there are times when I would endorse this preferred method of crushing spices, those used in jerk cooking are so flavorsome that I find a food mill can be substituted for the more old-fashioned instrument without detriment to their taste.

SERVES 4 TO 6

4 to 6 chicken breasts, about 1½ to 2½ pounds total

THE RUB
2 medium-size onions, chopped
2 tablespoons dark brown sugar
4 teaspoons ground allspice
2 teaspoons ground black pepper
2 teaspoons ground cayenne pepper
1 teaspoon ground cinnamon
1 teaspoon ground nutmeg

THE SAUCE

2 cups chicken stock or 2 chicken bouillon cubes dissolved in
   2 cups water
⅓ cup molasses
2 tablespoons tamarind concentrate
1 tablespoon minced fresh gingerroot
a sliver of Habanero chili (optional)

Start the fire in your smoker about 1½ to 2 hours before dinner-time. While the coals are heating, turn your attention to the chicken.

Rinse the chicken breasts and pat them dry with a paper towel. Set them out on a platter that will give you some working room when you're seasoning them.

Put the onion, brown sugar, allspice, black and cayenne peppers, cinnamon, and nutmeg in a food mill and mix until you have a rough paste.

Rub the paste into the chicken breasts, coating them thoroughly. You'll find that even after you've covered the chicken pieces lavishly in spices, there will be some rub left. Scoop it off the platter into a small bowl and reserve it for the sauce.

Transfer the chicken breasts one at a time to a piece of waxed paper laid out on your cutting board or butcher block. Cover the chicken with a second sheet of paper, then, using the smooth side of a meat mallet, whack the chicken breast until it's about half as thick as it was when you started and the seasoning is well impressed into it.

Add some wet smoking wood to the fire pan of your smoker and transfer the chicken from the waxed paper to the grill, placing about half the reserved rub in the smoker's water pan along with the hot water before putting the lid on the cooker.

Smoke the breasts for 1 to 1½ hours, keeping the cooking temperature between 200 and 220 degrees F.

While the chicken is smoking, start the sauce to go with it. Pour the chicken stock or bouillon into a small stainless steel or flame-proof ceramic saucepan and add the reserved rub along with the molasses, tamarind concentrate, and ginger. Stir well and simmer until the sauce is reduced by about one-half.

For those with an asbestos mouth, a smidgen of Habanero chili can be added, as it is in Jamaica. But be careful with this one. It really is dangerously hot. Serve the pungent sauce on the side.

CHICKEN SNAPS

T he one drawback — if such it can be called — of smoke cooking is that it forces you to slow down and take life easy. Because many smoked dishes call for marinating as well as leisurely cooking, some would argue that it also precludes spontaneity. Well, here's a smoked delight that calls for just a few simple seasonings from your spice shelf and goes from lighting the charcoal to a pleased palate in a little over an hour. Sliced chicken breasts cook very quickly.

If chicken breasts are not available sliced at the meat counter of your local supermarket or if you don't want to spend the extra money to have them carved for you, regular chicken breasts pounded flat or cut at an angle into thin cutlets work just as well.

Also, if you have one of those small-holed porcelain-clad steel racks like the Grill Topper, designed to keep small barbecue pieces or tender cuts from falling through to the drip pan, this would be a good time to use it.

SERVES 3 TO 4

> 1 to 2 pounds chicken breasts, whole or sliced
> 1 tablespoon sugar
> 1 tablespoon onion powder
> 1 tablespoon paprika
> 1 tablespoon ground black pepper
> 1 teaspoon ground cayenne pepper
> 1 teaspoon ground cumin
> ½ teaspoon salt

Start a fire in your smoker first thing so that it will be hot when the chicken is ready to go on the grill.

Rinse the chicken breasts and pat them dry with a paper towel. If they're not presliced, cut them at an angle into thin cutlets or lay them on a cutting board and pound them flat with the smooth side of a meat mallet.

In a small bowl, mix together the sugar, onion powder, paprika, black and cayenne peppers, cumin, and salt. Dust both sides of the chicken slices with the seasoning and let them absorb the spices for the 20 minutes or so it takes to get a good bed of coals glowing in your smoker.

Add a generous amount of wet smoking wood to the coals; fill the water pan halfway, remembering to use hot water so that you'll have a dense cloud of water vapor quickly; and arrange the chicken slices on the grill or its topper. Cover the cooker and smoke the chicken for 30 to 45 minutes at 200 to 220 degrees F.

Delicious straight from the grill, these little chicken bits have a snappy flavor all their own. They're even better accented with black cherry sauce.

BLACK CHERRY SAUCE

The first time I served smoked chicken with this sauce, it was received with considerable approbation by my family. "This is good!" Susan remarked as she poured more over her serving of chicken snaps. "What is it?"

"Orange juice, butter, Worcestershire sauce, black cherry preserves," I replied.

She stopped pouring for a moment. "You may have to defend that one."

"What do you mean?"

"Well, it tastes great. But no one's going to try it after reading the recipe and seeing that combination of ingredients."

"You don't eat with your mind," I pointed out.

Dear reader, you have been warned about appearances. It really turns out to be a great sauce.

MAKES APPROXIMATELY 1 CUP

> 4 tablespoons unsalted butter
> 1 cup orange juice
> 2 tablespoons black cherry preserves, preferably Chambord
> 1 tablespoon Worcestershire sauce

Melt the butter in a small stainless steel or flameproof ceramic saucepan set over low heat. Add the orange juice, black cherry preserves, and Worcestershire sauce. Whip the sauce until well blended, then simmer for 10 minutes, stirring occasionally. Serve in a small pitcher or gravy boat with the chicken snaps and let people help themselves.

BERBERÉ WINGS

Hot wings, in one form or another, have become quite the rage in recent years, particularly in college communities oversaturated with pizza. This version has a distinctive accent all its own.

Berberé is the spicy, incredibly hot paste that so distinguishes Ethiopian cooking. I first came upon it in New York a few years ago, when, following Langer's Rule of Restaurants, Ethiopian eating establishments began to appear there. Langer's Rule of Restaurants, in case you're not familiar with it, states that two years after a revolution or other political turmoil strikes a country anywhere in the world, restaurants of that particular culture begin opening in New York City.

Like catsup, *berberé* has many different formulations and in its homeland is used generously, indeed profligately, in and on a broad variety of dishes. Pan-cooking the spices for the paste before adding the liquids helps to bring out their flavors, but under no circumstances should you inhale the fumes while heating the spices. The aroma can be quite literally overwhelming.

SERVES 6 TO 8 AS AN APPETIZER, 2 TO 4 AS AN ENTRÉE

24 chicken wings, about 5 pounds total
¼ cup paprika
2 tablespoons ground black pepper
1 tablespoon ground cayenne pepper
1 tablespoon crushed red pepper
1 tablespoon chili powder
1 tablespoon dry mustard
1 tablespoon salt
2 teaspoons ground coriander
2 teaspoons ground turmeric
2 teaspoons ground ginger
1 teaspoon freshly ground cardamom seeds, white hulls
  discarded
1 teaspoon crushed star anise
1 teaspoon ground allspice
1 teaspoon ground cinnamon
1 teaspoon ground nutmeg
1 teaspoon ground cloves
½ teaspoon crushed fenugreek
⅓ cup red wine
⅓ cup peanut oil
3 tablespoons lemon juice

This dish requires overnight marinating before cooking, so prepare the chicken and the paste for it the day before you plan to serve the wings.

Using poultry shears or a cleaver, separate the chicken wings at the first joint. You can cut off the wing tips and discard them, since there's very little meat past the second joint, but I leave them on, both because doing so saves work and because they're an extra nibble.

To make the *berberé,* set on the stove a large cast-iron or other heavy nonaluminum frying pan in which you'll be able to spread out the combined spices in a relatively thin layer. Measure into the pan the paprika, black and cayenne peppers, crushed red pepper, chili powder, dry mustard, salt, coriander, turmeric, ginger, cardamom, crushed anise, allspice, cinnamon, nutmeg, cloves, and fenugreek. Lightly toast the spices over medium heat, stirring to make sure they don't burn or blacken.

Add the wine to the pan slowly, stirring constantly to blend the spices and the liquid. Still stirring, cook the mixture over low heat for about 2 minutes. You should end up with a uniform dryish paste, although it will be gritty, not smooth.

Remove the pan from heat and add the peanut oil and lemon juice. Blend well.

Place the wings in the pan and push them around with a fork until they are well coated with the *berberé*. Then transfer the wings to a nonreactive bowl with a tight-fitting cover or a self-sealing Ziploc-type plastic bag and refrigerate overnight.

The following day, start a good bed of coals going in your smoker about 1¼ hours before you plan to serve the wings. Add wet wood to the fire pan and hot water to the water pan when the coals are good and hot.

Smoke the wings, covered, for 45 minutes at 210 to 230 degrees F. Serve piping hot from the grill.

HOT FOOT

H ere's a variation on the theme of hot wings that's a bit more substantial than the usual nibble, using the meatier drumsticks. Plenty hot 'n' spicy, it lets you taste the chicken as well as the heat.

SERVES 3 TO 4

12 to 16 chicken drumsticks, about 2½ to 3½ pounds total
¼ cup flour
2 teaspoons paprika
1 teaspoon ground black pepper
1 teaspoon ground white pepper
1 teaspoon ground cayenne pepper
1 teaspoon ground thyme
1 teaspoon garlic powder
1 teaspoon salt

The day before you plan to serve these drumsticks, lay them out on a cutting board or butcher block and pierce them all over with a fork so that, when they are seasoned, the spices will permeate the meat nicely. Set aside.

Measure into a Ziploc-type plastic bag the flour; paprika; black, white, and cayenne peppers; thyme; garlic powder; and salt. Close the bag and shake to blend the spices well.

Add the drumsticks to the bag, zip it shut again, and shake until the drumsticks are thoroughly coated with the seasoning. Refrigerate overnight.

The following day, about 2 hours before dinnertime, fire up your smoker and, when the coals are glowing, add some wet wood to the fire pan and fill the water pan halfway with hot water. Transfer the drumsticks from their bag to the grill and cover the smoker snugly.

Smoke at 200 to 220 degrees F. for about 1½ hours, or until the juice runs clear when the meat is pricked and the drums are lusciously tender.

MARYLAND LEGS

T he sea meets the sky all along the Maryland estuaries, which may be why the state is renowned for one dish from each of those environs — namely, Maryland crab and Maryland chicken. All right, so modern-day chickens have about as much chance of reaching the sky as a lead zeppelin does. I'm talking origins here.

The following recipe traces its lineage to the crab boil, but in this instance the spices traditional to that feast have been transposed to chicken and smoking has supplanted steaming. The mingled heritage makes for a very tasty repast.

SERVES 6 TO 8

24 *chicken drumsticks, about 5 pounds total*
3 *tablespoons dry mustard*
2 *tablespoons celery salt*
2 *tablespoons paprika*
2 *tablespoons ground black pepper*
2 *teaspoons ground ginger*
1 *teaspoon ground cloves*
1 *bay leaf, finely crushed*

The day before you plan to serve the chicken legs, set out a Ziploc-type plastic bag large enough to hold all the drumsticks with some room to spare. Pierce the drumsticks all over with a fork to let the seasoning in. Set aside.

Measure into the bag the dry mustard, celery salt, paprika, pepper, ginger, cloves, and crushed bay leaf. Close and shake the bag to mix the spices thoroughly. Add the drumsticks, seal the bag well, and shake again to coat all the chicken pieces evenly with the spice blend. Refrigerate overnight.

The following day, start a fire in your smoker about 2 to 2½ hours before dinnertime, build up a good bed of coals, and fill the water pan halfway with hot water. Add some wet smoking wood, arrange the chicken legs on the grill. Before discarding the bag, shake any leftover spices from it into the smoker's water pan for extra flavor.

Smoke the drums under a tight cooker lid at 200 to 220 degrees F. for 1½ to 2 hours, turning them after the first 45 minutes to 1 hour.

LINGUICA-STUFFED CHICKEN THIGHS

T his dish combines a bit of everything culinary from Portugal to Penang by way of North America. It's particularly popular with kids. Even fussy eaters often ask for seconds, so it's ideal for a family cookout with several generations in attendance.

From Portugal comes the linguica, the coarse, pungent Iberian sausage now available in many specialty stores and larger supermarkets across the country. Traditionally, linguica sausages are grilled over charcoal, and wood smoke enhances their flavor. The chicken thighs are by now as American as apple pie, while the peanut-based sauce is a derivative of the satay accompaniment so widely associated with Asia. All in all, this is a world-class dish in every sense of the term.

SERVES 6

6 boneless roasting chicken thighs, about 2 pounds total
6 linguica sausages
1 small onion, quartered
2 cloves garlic, peeled
1 to 2 dried whole chilies
2 tablespoons pine nuts
1 tablespoon lemon zest
1 teaspoon sugar
1 cup crunchy peanut butter
1 tablespoon peanut oil
1 cup coconut milk

Start your preparations for the stuffed thighs about 2 hours before dinnertime. Set out a shallow dish just large enough to hold the chicken thighs, rather snugly once they've been stuffed with the sausages. You'll want to put a layer of sauce in the dish before you wedge the thighs into it, though, so make the peanut sauce before you do the actual stuffing.

Place in a food processor the onion, garlic, chilies, pine nuts, lemon zest, sugar, and, on top of it all, the peanut butter. Puree until smooth. Add the oil in a slow stream, blending well.

Transfer the puree to a small stainless steel or flameproof ceramic saucepan. Stir in the coconut milk and bring to a boil. Simmer for 5 minutes, stirring constantly. Set aside to cool somewhat.

Open up the chicken thighs — they will be slit along one side from being boned — and lay them on a cutting board. Using the smooth side of a meat mallet, pound the thighs to flatten them.

Place a linguica sausage in the center of each thigh and wrap the chicken around it. Pin the thighs together with poultry-lacing skewers. Remember to remove them before serving, though.

Put a little of the peanut sauce in the dish you've set out, wedge the stuffed chicken thighs into the dish, and pour the rest of the sauce over them. Allow the chicken to steep briefly in the warm liquid while you get the coals going in the smoker. The puree is not a true marinade in the usual sense of the word, lacking as it does an acidic component, but the flavor of the sauce will seep into the chicken.

Once the smoker is going well, add some wet wood to the fire pan and hot water to the water pan, transfer the thighs to the grill, reserving the sauce, and put the lid on the cooker. Smoke the stuffed thighs at 200 to 220 degrees F. for about 1 hour, or until done.

When the chicken is almost ready, reheat the peanut puree in its saucepan and simmer for a few minutes. Serve as a dipping sauce.

TURKEY THIGHS WITH FRESH MOZZARELLA

urkey's two traditional places on the American table used to be at holiday feasts and in hot turkey sandwiches with mashed potatoes and gravy. Recently, however, turkey producers, goaded by the marketing success of rival chicken ranchers, have brought a whole line of turkey specials to supermarket poultry counters. From burgers to sausages to various precut parts designed to reduce these large birds to more manageable proportions for today's smaller families, turkey is being touted as prudent, low-fat, good-for-you fare.

Well, turkey can have a lot of flavor, too. A piece of dark meat, a bit of cheese, an herby baste, and a long smoke add up to a tasty delight indeed.

Like most people, I don't always have half a cup of good chicken stock sitting around in the fridge or freezer just waiting for a recipe calling for it. For this dish, a chicken bouillon cube dissolved in half a cup of hot water works fine as a substitute.

SERVES 1 — MULTIPLY BY THE NUMBER OF PERSONS TO BE SERVED

1 turkey thigh, skin on, about 1 pound

THE POCKET STUFFING
2 balls fresh mozzarella cheese, about ¼ pound total, sliced into ¼-inch-thick rounds
2 tablespoons pesto

THE BASTE
½ cup concentrated chicken stock or 1 chicken bouillon cube dissolved in ½ cup boiling water
½ cup white wine
6 tablespoons tomato paste
2 tablespoons pesto
2 tablespoons olive oil

About 3½ to 4½ hours before you want to serve this dish, start a fire in your smoker and get a good bed of coals established. Then turn your attention to the turkey.

The skin of the turkey thigh will lift away from the meat more easily along one edge than the other. Where it does, work your fingers under it and separate the skin from the meat over the whole top of the thigh, forming a pocket. Make sure to leave the skin attached at the edge farthest from your fingers as well as at the sides.

Fill the pocket with the mozzarella slices. Then spoon the pesto between the cheese and the thigh. Set the dressed thigh aside while you prepare the basting sauce.

In a small stainless steel or flameproof ceramic saucepan, mix together the chicken stock or bouillon, wine, tomato paste, pesto, and olive oil. Stir until well blended. Bring to a boil and simmer for 5 minutes to thicken the sauce a bit.

Add some wet wood to your smoker's fire pan and some hot water to the water pan, then place the thigh on the grill, stuffed side up, and baste the top with the sauce.

Smoke for 3 to 4 hours at 220 to 240 degrees F., basting well every 30 to 45 minutes and checking the wet wood and water supplies occasionally while you have the lid off the smoker.

PRESSED CORNISH GAME HEN

It's amazing the ignobility to which a teenage son can reduce an elegant entrée. This dish started out to be a smoked version of Russian pressed squab. Lacking both the squab and the appropriate press, I resorted to Cornish game hens and a cast-iron skillet. Both served their surrogate role admirably. Upon my presentation of the finished product, Revell, subjected to an endless stream of experimentation during the researching of this book, greeted my efforts with the cheerful comment, "Ah, and what do we have here, Dad, smoked fresh road kill?"

In classic cuisine, one of the purposes of pressing squab is supposedly to ensure a crisp layer of skin. This particular end is not achieved by smoke cooking. Crispness demands a certain dryness, the very antithesis of the celebrated accomplishments of slow, moist, indirect cooking.

Another objective of pressing is to yield a more tender, succulent dish. Here the formula succeeds beyond all expectations, abetted spectacularly by the smoking process.

SERVES 2

> 2 Cornish game hens, 1¼ to 1½ pounds each
> 2 tablespoons dried rosemary, divided
> 2 teaspoons white peppercorns
> 1 teaspoon black peppercorns
> 1 teaspoon coarse kosher or sea salt

Rinse the Cornish hens briefly under running water, drain, pat dry with a paper towel, and lay the birds on a large cutting board or butcher block. Using poultry shears or a cleaver, cut along both sides of the backbone of each hen, taking care not to slice all the way through to the other side. You want the breastbone intact to serve as a hinge, allowing you to fold out the two halves of the fowl. Remove the backbone and neck extension of each bird.

Open the fowl so they lie flat and place them skin side up on the board or block. Now pick up a heavy skillet — I use a 10½-inch cast-iron model that weighs in at around 5 pounds — and let the hens have it, forcefully, a number of times. You should be able to reduce their thickness by about one-half.

Measure 1 tablespoon of the rosemary, the white and black peppercorns, and the salt into a mortar and grind them with a pestle until none of the bits are larger than pinheads. A food mill or an electric coffee grinder dedicated to spices instead of coffee beans will do the job, too, but while I don't want to sound like a dreadful spice snob, the mortar and pestle honestly do it better. You gain a more fragrant mix using the old-fashioned utensil. I'm not sure why,

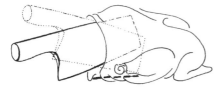

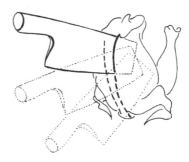

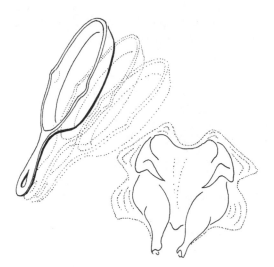

but my guess is that the quick grind of a coffee mill warms the spices enough so that some of the volatile oils are lost.

Rub the freshly ground spices liberally into both sides of the hens, then let them rest at room temperature while you fire up your smoker.

Once the coals in the fire pan have settled down to a steady smolder, add some wet smoking wood, fill the water pan with hot water, and sprinkle 1 teaspoon of the remaining rosemary over the water. Place the hens, skin side up, on the grill and weight each of them with a cast-iron skillet or a foil-wrapped brick.

Smoke the game hens, tightly covered by the cooker lid, at 200 to 220 degrees F. for 45 minutes. Then turn them so that they are skin side down on the grill, sprinkle the remaining 2 teaspoons of rosemary over the coals, and smoke the hens for another 30 to 45 minutes.

To serve, cut the hens in half before arranging them attractively on a platter.

ORANGE-GLAZED GAME HEN WITH WATERCRESS STUFFING

T he bittersweet of a good orange marmalade is the perfect foil for the peppery punch of watercress in the dressing used here. The cress stuffing also productively disposes of those last spoonfuls of wild rice left in a bowl at the back of the bottommost shelf of the fridge — the ones that weren't quite finished off as a midnight snack. The key to achieving the nicest contrast between the piquant stuffing and the fruit-spiced glaze lies in the marmalade. It should be one that's not too sweet.

The recipe can be adapted — up to the capacity of your grill, that is — to accommodate any number of guests. Plan on one Cornish game hen per person.

SERVES 1 — MULTIPLY BY THE NUMBER OF PERSONS TO BE SERVED

> 1 Cornish game hen
> pepper to taste
> salt to taste

THE STUFFING

> 1 cup cooked wild rice
> 1 cup coarsely chopped fresh watercress
> 2 scallions, greens included, finely chopped
> 1 tablespoon butter, melted
> hearty splash of Tabasco or similar hot red pepper sauce

THE GLAZE

> 4 tablespoons butter
> 3 tablespoons orange marmalade, preferably Seville
> 1 tablespoon lemon juice

Fire up your smoker 3½ to 4 hours before dinnertime so the coals will be ready when you are.

Rinse the game hen briefly under running water, drain, and pat dry with a paper towel. Salt and pepper the hen inside and out.

In a small bowl, mix together the wild rice, watercress, and scallions for the stuffing. Add the butter and Tabasco or other hot red pepper sauce.

Stuff the hen generously, for this stuffing does not swell with cooking. It's not necessary to tie the legs together, but some folks like to do so out of tradition.

For the glaze, melt the butter in a small saucepan and stir in the marmalade and lemon juice.

Add some wet wood to the fire pan of your smoker and place the Cornish hen on the grill breast up over a pan of hot water. Brush liberally with glaze before putting the cooker lid on.

Smoke the hen at 200 to 220 degrees F. for 2 to 2½ hours. Then slather on lots more of the glazing liquid and smoke for 30 minutes more. It will be burnished to golden perfection.

MARINATED MUSHROOMS

There's something about delicately marinated mushrooms that makes them a perfect foil for smoked dishes, particularly fowl, and even more particularly the little Cornish hens. Then too, the sheer mycological variety seen on supermarket shelves today renders almost irresistible the temptation to find more excuses for bringing home the fascinating fungi. So here's a dish that provides a good reason to do just that, while at the same time supplying a wonderful accompaniment to your smoked fare. It can be made well in advance — in fact gains flavor with mellowing — and the venture can be fitted in at your leisure. Marinated mushrooms are awfully nice to have on hand when something a little special is wanted for a company dinner.

Any and all of the newly available varieties of mushrooms, from crimini to oyster, work well with the recipe given here. Mix and match for added flavor.

MAKES ABOUT 4 CUPS

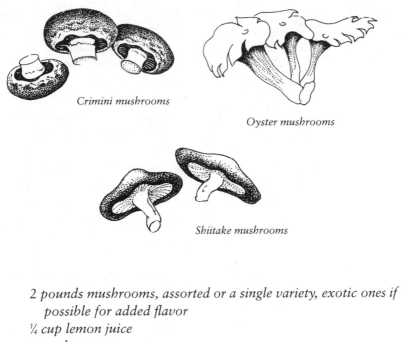

Crimini mushrooms

Oyster mushrooms

Shiitake mushrooms

2 pounds mushrooms, assorted or a single variety, exotic ones if
  possible for added flavor
¼ cup lemon juice
sea salt to taste
1½ cups broth reserved from cooking the mushrooms
½ cup tarragon vinegar
2 tablespoons sugar
20 black peppercorns
3 bay leaves
6 cloves garlic, peeled and very thinly sliced
10 fresh sprigs dill
4 scallions, greens included, minced
olive oil

Clean the mushrooms by wiping them with a paper towel or, if
you rinse your mushrooms, pat them good and dry. Slice off and
discard the very bottoms of the stems if they're tough. Cut in half
any large mushrooms, say ones over 2 inches in diameter. Flat
mushrooms such as shiitakes can be cut into ½-inch strips for visual
variety. However you cut them, though, bear in mind that the mushrooms will be reduced in size by almost one-half after cooking, so
don't make the pieces too small.

Sprinkle the mushrooms with the lemon juice, toss, and let rest
for 15 minutes or so. Then place them in a large stainless steel or

flameproof ceramic saucepan. Don't use aluminum or cast iron, as these metals will react with the acidic lemon juice.

Add enough water to the pan so that the mushrooms are half-covered with liquid — use at least 1½ cups — and bring to a boil. Reduce the heat to a simmer and cook, stirring occasionally, for 10 minutes. By then the mushrooms will be reduced to the point where they will be almost covered by the liquid. Sprinkle with the salt, then fish the mushrooms out with a slotted stainless steel or wooden spoon.

The cooking broth remaining in the pan will form the base for the marinade. Traditionally, it was filtered through a few layers of cheesecloth to clarify it before mixing it with the other ingredients. In our house, we make our coffee using a Melitta carafe and filter, and I've found that combination a splendid device for straining liquids like this.

However you do your filtering, strain 1½ cups of the mushroom liquid into a pot, again making sure it's a nonreactive one. The pot in which the mushrooms were cooked works fine if it's rinsed out so no small particles remain to cloud the pickling liquid.

Add the vinegar, sugar, peppercorns, and bay leaves to the broth and simmer, covered, for about 10 minutes.

Let both the mushrooms and the marinade cool to room temperature. Meanwhile, mix together the garlic, dill, and scallions.

In a very clean quart jar — old mayonnaise jars are perfect for this — alternate layers of mushrooms with the garlic, dill, and scallion mixture. Leave a little space at the top of the jar.

Slowly pour the liquid marinade, minus the bay leaves, into the container. Lay the three bay leaves in a star pattern on top and pour a thin layer of olive oil over them as a cover.

Cap the jar and place it in the refrigerator for at least a week. Give the mushrooms 2 weeks to mellow and they'll be even tastier. If you must, you can sneak a sample the day after you put the mushrooms to steep. But waiting is really worth it.

9. SEA SMOKE

Seafood and smoke go together like a rocky coast and fog, and the combination is almost as ancient. Peat fires and seaweed often flavored fish in windswept coastal areas where trees were stunted and scarce. Farther inland, where salmon and other migratory species made their way by fast-flowing watercourses, whatever grew along the riverbanks provided the fuel. The underlying constant was a meal with a very special savor.

Almost all the sea's bounty smokes well and, as with meat, is not easy to overcook to a dried shingle when you're using a water smoker. The one exception here seems to be shrimp, which for some reason does lose its succulence if provoked by too long a stay on the grill, even one surrounded by plenty of moisture. So when you smoke shrimp, you'll just have to keep taste-testing it occasionally to check the degree of doneness. Ah, the rough life of a smoke chef.

NEOLITHIC MUSSELS

While teaching English in China, an old friend and fellow writer, the novelist Robert Abel, came upon a restaurant curiously named the Neolithic. Not your ordinary Beijing restaurant, this establishment features only food cooked by burning-hot stones.

The stones, hotter than charcoal briquettes and handled with tongs, serve as the heating element in all manner of cooking, including smoking, where pine needles are sometimes used for the flavor. Abe found the Neolithic's smoked mussels particularly delicious. Trying to duplicate them at home, he pressed into service his covered grill and a bamboo basket from a Chinese steamer. This led to bamboo-flavored mussels, as the basket caught fire.

The following recipe evolved after somewhat further circuitous modification by both Abe and myself.

SERVES 8 TO 10 AS AN APPETIZER, 3 TO 4 AS AN ENTRÉE

4 pounds mussels in the shell
1 teaspoon freshly ground cardamom seeds, white hulls discarded
1 teaspoon ground thyme
1 teaspoon ground cumin

About an hour before the appetizer or the dinner course, as the case may be, start a fire in your smoker. While the coals are settling, scrub and debeard the mussels, pulling out any Brillo pad–like seaweed grasped in the bivalve's shell.

For the next step, you can use a traditional wooden Chinese steamer, a fairly large version of its domestic equivalent, or a nonreactive colander set inside a big covered pot. Heat the appropriate amount of water in the bottom of the steamer. Add the cardamom, thyme, and cumin to the water and the mussels to the container above it, cover the pot, and steam the mollusks over medium heat for 5 minutes or until they open. Discard any that do not.

Add some soaked dense wood such as hickory to the coals in your smoker's fire pan, then pour the herby water from the steamer into the smoker's water pan, topping it off, if need be, with more hot water. Transfer the opened mussels to the grill, resting them on the hinged side of their shells so that they're cupped.

Smoke the mussels, snug under the cooker's lid, at 210 to 230 degrees F. for 15 to 30 minutes.

SMOKED SMELTS

D elightful as a finger-food appetizer, smoked smelts are also a tasty entrée, particularly if accompanied by hot, freshly mashed new potatoes and peas plucked from the garden not an hour before. These tiny fish are now available dressed from most fishmongers and supermarket fish counters, making them about as easy to prepare as they could possibly be.

SERVES 4 AS AN APPETIZER, 2 AS AN ENTRÉE

1 pound dressed smelts
2 tablespoons olive oil
pepper to taste
salt to taste

Start building up hot coals in your smoker about 1½ hours before you want to serve these little fish.

Rinse the smelts quickly in a stainless steel colander held under running water and drain them well, shaking the colander gently until the excess water has dripped through the perforations.

Dribble the olive oil over the fish and toss them in the colander with a rotating motion until they are nicely coated with the oil. Sprinkle liberally with pepper, a little less generously with salt. Toss again.

Small smelts are in danger of slipping between the bars of some, if indeed not most, barbecue grills. Since what you're after here is smoked fish, not smelts simmered in the water pan, you want to avoid that eventuality. There are a couple of ways to tackle the problem.

For one thing, you can use two racks, setting one on top of the other and turning it until its rods are at right angles to those of the lower one, making a grid of small squares. Alternatively, you can replace your regular grill with one of those porcelain-clad steel racks featuring small perforated holes instead of the parallel bars traditional on barbecue grills.

When you've settled on the grill arrangement you're going to use, put some wet wood in your smoker's fire pan, pour some hot water into the water pan, and you'll be ready to cook the smelts. In transferring them to the grill, make sure you spread them out adequately. It's all right for them to be touching, but don't pile them two or three deep, or you'll end up with some rare fish indeed.

Put the lid on the cooker and smoke the smelts at 200 to 220 degrees F. for 1 hour if you like them soft and golden, longer if you like them browned and chewy-crisp.

MÁLAGA SHRIMP

M ore and more, beer is being used as a cooking liquid, contributing both moisture and a subtle, rich flavor to steamed and simmered fare. Increasingly, too, it forms the base of marinades, where the enzymatic interaction it provokes is reputed to improve the tenderness of tougher cuts. Having not exactly excelled in biochemistry during my college days, I won't argue the point one way or the other. I do find that beer, like wine, adds a certain nuance of its own to a number of dishes, particularly hearty ones. When all is said and done, though, I usually prefer to drink my beer and eat my food.

There are some morsels that seem inherently natural accompaniments to a nice cold brew. I can remember many a delightful afternoon spent with friends in a quiet little bar on the waterfront in Málaga, leisurely quaffing *cervecas* and peeling shrimp. By the end of the day, there would be a small mountain of crustacean exoskeletons on the floor beneath each of our stools. When we wandered in the following afternoon, the shells would be gone, and so we would have to begin building our mountains anew. Somebody had to do it, we told ourselves with the enthusiasm that only a surfeit of college studies and the mighty dollar of the early sixties could between them muster. As I recall, a plate of 6 large shrimp and a beer cost 10 cents.

SERVES 1 — MULTIPLY BY THE NUMBER OF PERSONS TO BE SERVED

1 pound (10 to 15) whole shrimp in the shell, heads left on
½ cup lime juice
½ cup molasses
¼ cup olive oil
1 tablespoon Worcestershire sauce
2 teaspoons Tabasco or similar hot red pepper sauce
1 teaspoon freshly ground cardamom seeds, white hulls
*   discarded*
1 teaspoon ground cayenne pepper
1 teaspoon ground ginger
1 teaspoon celery seed
½ teaspoon ground nutmeg

A day in advance of cooking the shrimp, prepare them for a long night's marinating. Using a small, sharp knife, cut through the shell of each shrimp along the belly line from head to tail. Work the split shell open so the marinade will be better able to penetrate, but don't peel the shrimp. You want the shell to cradle the spicy liquid.

Pour the lime juice, molasses, and olive oil into a large mixing bowl suitable for marinating and add the Worcestershire sauce and Tabasco or other hot red pepper sauce. Blend the liquid ingredients well, then whisk in the cardamom, cayenne pepper, ginger, celery seed, and nutmeg, making sure any clumps of spices are dissolved.

Add the shrimp to the bowl, stir to coat well with the marinade, cover tightly with plastic wrap, and refrigerate overnight. Stir again the following morning.

About 1 hour before you want to serve the shrimp, start a fire in the smoker, get a good bed of coals going, and add some wet wood and a pan of hot water. When the smoker is registering 200 to 230 degrees F., settle the shrimp on the grill. Reserve the marinade for basting.

Fit the lid on the cooker and smoke the shrimp for 30 to 45 minutes, checking that the smoker stays between 200 and 230 degrees F. and brushing the shrimp liberally with the reserved marinade every 10 minutes or so. A lot of marinade will dribble through the grill into the water pan, but no matter. It will just add more fragrance to the moisture enveloping the shrimp. Make sure that you don't overcook the shrimp, or they'll become tough. The best way to check is by sampling.

Serve the shrimp hot from the smoker with plenty of beer and big napkins.

SHRIMP ORIENTAL

Coriander by any other name is still *Coriandrum sativum,* but it may be on an entirely different part of the menu and not immediately identifiable as being the same herb. Coriander is used as a flavoring agent in sausages, pickles, and various baked goods — diverse foods, yes, but united in their use of the seed. The leaf of the young herb is used in cooking as well, but here it more often goes by the name Chinese parsley or, more recently, the yuppie appellation cilantro.

It's in Oriental cooking, in all manner of soups and savory dishes, that cilantro excels. The distinctive flavor of the tender leaves particularly enhances fish and shellfish such as shrimp, remarkably so when combined with lime juice.

When buying shrimp for the grill, remember that very small shellfish require a special grill accessory or a double grill to keep them from slipping through the cracks to simmer in the water pan — or worse.

SERVES 4

2 pounds (32 to 40) whole shrimp in the shell
1 cup lightly packed fresh mint leaves, stemmed
1 cup lightly packed fresh cilantro, stemmed
2 cups lime juice
½ cup molasses
½ cup coconut milk

The day before you want to serve this dish, rinse and peel the shrimp. You can devein them, too, but, frankly, I never bother, and no one seems to notice. It's not really necessary when the shrimp are to be marinated or smoked. Place the dressed shrimp in a nonreactive bowl or pan large enough to accommodate them with their marinade. Set aside.

Liquefy the mint and cilantro leaves in a blender or food processor. Add the lime juice, molasses, and coconut milk and mix lightly until well blended.

Pour the marinade over the shrimp and stir gently to coat each shellfish well. Refrigerate, tightly covered with plastic wrap, overnight, stirring once lightly before going to bed if you happen to remember. Stir again in the morning.

About 1 hour before dinnertime, remove the shrimp from the refrigerator to finish marinating at room temperature. Fire up the smoker and, once a good bed of coals is established, add some wet wood to the fire pan and hot water to the water pan.

Transfer the shrimp to the grill — or, if they seem to be in danger of falling through the bars, to two grills placed crosswise one atop the other to form a grid. Alternatively, lay the shrimp on one of those porcelain-clad steel grill trays designed specifically for small items, oiling it lightly first. In either case, when you've moved the shrimp from their bowl or pan, reserve the marinade.

Cover the cooker and smoke the shrimp at 220 to 240 degrees F. for 20 to 30 minutes, or until just pink and white and tender, opening the smoker only to turn and baste them after the first 10 minutes and again after another 5 to 10 minutes.

Heat the reserved marinade in a small stainless steel or flameproof ceramic saucepan for 3 minutes and serve in bowls as a dipping sauce.

CAJUN TUNA STEAK

T una has undergone quite a transformation in American cooking over the past decade, exalted from its former status as a canned standby in the sandwich and casserole division to prominence on the au courant grill of the nineties. This observation is in no way meant to denigrate the palatable comfort of a good tuna salad sandwich on toast with garden-ripe tomatoes and lettuce. Nonetheless, fresh tuna is altogether different fare. Dense, solid, steaklike in texture, it lends itself particularly well to smoking. Being a fish with rather forceful flavor as well, tuna also accepts the boldness of Cajun spicing without being overcome by it.

A common practice is to sear tuna in a hot skillet to seal in the juices and flavor before grilling it. Smoking eliminates the need for this step, saving a bit of dishwashing — the reduction of which, rarely mentioned in cookbooks, is one of the real boons of smoke cooking.

SERVES 4

4 boneless tuna steaks about 1 inch thick, 8 to 10 ounces each
¼ cup olive oil
½ cup white vinegar
½ cup water
1 tablespoon molasses
1 tablespoon tomato paste
1 teaspoon Worcestershire sauce
1 teaspoon Tabasco or similar hot red pepper sauce
2 cloves garlic, peeled and put through a garlic press
1 tablespoon paprika
1 teaspoon ground cayenne pepper
1 teaspoon ground black pepper
1 teaspoon ground thyme
½ teaspoon ground coriander

You'll need to start the preliminary preparations for this dish about 3 hours before dinnertime. Set out a shallow nonreactive pan or platter large and deep enough to hold the tuna steaks.

In a small mixing bowl, combine the olive oil, vinegar, water, molasses, tomato paste, Worcestershire sauce, and Tabasco or other hot red pepper sauce. Blend these liquid ingredients until smooth.

Add the garlic and stir. Then whisk in the paprika, cayenne and black peppers, thyme, and coriander, making sure any clumps of the spices are pressed out against the edge of the bowl.

Pour the marinade into the pan or platter and place the tuna steaks in the liquid. Turn them several times to coat well on all sides, piercing the fish with a fork in several places as you go.

Let the steaks marinate, loosely covered, at room temperature for 2 hours. About 30 minutes before the end of that time, start your smoker fire. Once the coals are established, add some well-soaked dense wood, such as hickory or maple, for the smoke flavor.

Brush the grill lightly with olive oil before slipping the steaks onto it. Smoke over a pan of hot water and under a tight lid at a temperature of 200 to 220 degrees F. for 30 to 45 minutes, the precise time depending on how well-done you like your fish. On the whole, tuna is better on the rare side.

TSUNAMI TUNA

ere's a fish all awash in Oriental flavor. Tuna is a popular sashimi or sushi selection, of course, presented simply with soy sauce and wasabi, the green Japanese horseradish paste. For that matter, the tuna quick-grilled as some chefs cook it these days might better be served as sashimi, since the scorched fish is quite often still cold in the middle.

It's true that you don't want to overcook tuna. Left on the grill too long, a tuna steak can become not only dry, but bitter as well. Fortunately, it's almost impossible to oversmoke this fish.

SERVES 4

> 4 tuna steaks, ½ to ¾ pound each
> 1 cup teriyaki sauce
> 1 cup sesame oil
> ½ cup rice vinegar
> 2 scallions, greens included, coarsely chopped
> toasted sesame seeds for garnish

About 1 hour before your fish course, place the tuna steaks in a nonreactive glass or ceramic dish large enough to accommodate them with a marinade.

To make the marinade, measure the teriyaki sauce, sesame oil, and vinegar into a blender or food processor. Add the scallions and mix until the scallions are reduced to match head–size pieces.

Pour the marinade over the tuna, turn the steaks in the sauce to cover well on both sides, and leave to steep while you light the smoker.

Once the coals are glowing in the cooker's fire pan and you've added enough wet wood so the smoke is billowing, brush your grill with oil and transfer the steaks to it, placing a pan of hot water beneath them.

Baste the fish with some of the extra liquid from the marinating dish and smoke, covered, at 190 to 210 degrees F. for 15 minutes. Keep the marinade warm meanwhile.

Turn the steaks and baste again with marinade before smoking for another 10 to 15 minutes. When the fish can be easily pierced with a fork, it's ready. Try not to open the smoker, though, except to turn the steaks the first time and to test them for doneness.

Brush the tuna with the last bit of sauce, brought to a simmer in a small nonreactive pan, and garnish with the sesame seeds.

HEAVENLY HALIBUT STEAK

Halibut is one of those delicately flavored delights all too easily overpowered by strong marinades or overcooking or, for that matter, smoke. By all means, use some chunks or chips of a mildly aromatic wood such as alder, maple, or pecan, but stay away from mesquite and even hickory.

SERVES 4 TO 6

> 3 halibut steaks, about 3 to 4 pounds total
> ½ cup lemon juice
> ⅓ cup olive oil
> ¼ cup water
> 1 cup loosely packed fresh parsley
> 1 teaspoon dry mustard
> 1 clove garlic, peeled and chopped
> 1 teaspoon ground black pepper
> ½ teaspoon salt

A day in advance of your halibut dinner, set out a nonreactive ceramic or glass dish large enough to hold the steaks plus their marinade.

Pour the lemon juice, olive oil, and water into a blender or food processor and add the parsley, dry mustard, garlic, pepper, and salt. Mix until the parsley is liquefied and the sauce is smooth. Drench the fish with the marinade, turning the steaks in the liquid to coat them on both sides. Refrigerate overnight tightly covered with plastic wrap, turning the halibut a couple of times when you think of it.

The following day, remove the fish from the refrigerator about 1½ hours before dinnertime and let it sit at room temperature while you fire up the smoker, add wet wood, and fill the water pan with hot water.

Once the smoker is billowing at 190 to 220 degrees F., lightly oil your grill, drain the steaks, and place them on the rack. Cover with the cooker lid and smoke for about 45 minutes, or until the halibut is done to your taste.

SMOKED SWORDFISH STEAK

G ood swordfish is great, but unfortunately a lot of it reaches the table overcooked and dry, giving it a less-than-palatable reputation. Here, once more, smoke cooking comes to the rescue, yielding moist, tender swordfish that can't be beat.

If you look closely at a swordfish steak, the most common cut of this fish, you'll notice whorls, or rings, much like those seen in a cross section of a tree. These whorls are an identifying mark assuring you that what you've procured is indeed swordfish. Some less-than-honest fishmongers are selling mako shark, which is far less expensive, under the swordfish label. No whorls, no swordfish.

SERVES 3 TO 4

2-pound swordfish steak
½ cup white wine
½ cup chicken stock or ½ chicken bouillon cube dissolved in
   ½ cup boiling water
⅓ cup olive oil
2 tablespoons tomato paste
3 cloves garlic, peeled and slivered
1 teaspoon dried rosemary, coarsely ground in a mortar and
   pestle
1 teaspoon ground thyme
½ teaspoon ground white pepper
½ teaspoon salt

The day before this dish is to be on the menu, set out a nonreactive glass or ceramic dish large and deep enough to hold the swordfish steak.

In a small mixing bowl, stir together the wine, chicken stock, and olive oil. Spoon in the tomato paste and beat until smooth. Sprinkle the garlic, rosemary, thyme, white pepper, and salt over the liquid ingredients and whisk well, making sure no clumps of spices remain.

Lay the swordfish steak in the dish and turn it over in the marinade to coat both sides. Let the steak marinate, tightly covered with plastic wrap, in the refrigerator overnight, turning it once or twice.

To smoke the swordfish, remove the steak from the refrigerator and let it rest at room temperature while you start the fire in your smoker. Once the coals are glowing in the fire pan, add wet wood and fill the water pan halfway with hot water. Oil the grill lightly, then transfer the fish from its marinade to the rack. Pour the marinade into a small stainless steel or flameproof ceramic saucepan and reserve.

Cover the smoker tightly with its lid and smoke the steak for 40 to 50 minutes at 190 to 210 degrees F.

About 10 minutes before taking the fish from the grill, bring the marinade to a simmer on the stove and let it cook slowly over low heat. Drizzle lightly over the swordfish steak just before serving.

SWORDFISH VIETNAMESE

Vietnamese food, with its shadings of Chinese and Thai cuisine, is beginning to make a definite culinary statement in the States. Beyond the popular noodle soup called *pho,* it includes a broad range of salad and vegetable dishes, often redolent of fresh basil and cilantro, and plenty of fish, which should come as no surprise considering the country's extensive coastline.

In the recipe given here, the only ingredient not generally procurable from today's well-stocked neighborhood grocery stores is the Vietnamese fish sauce *nouc mam.* However, this catsup of the Orient may be found on the shelves of any Asian food store, and a bottle lasts a long time.

SERVES 2

1¼- to 1½-pound swordfish steak, halved
2 tablespoons nouc mam
1½ teaspoons finely minced fresh gingerroot
1 teaspoon ground turmeric
½ teaspoon ground black pepper
2 scallions, greens included, finely minced
½ cup chopped fresh cilantro
¼ cup chopped fresh basil

About 1½ hours before dinnertime, set the swordfish steak out on a platter or a plate large enough to permit the pieces to be turned.

In a small mixing bowl, combine the *nouc mam,* ginger, turmeric, and pepper. Brush this mixture over the fish, turn, and brush the other side. Let rest while you start a fire in the smoker, build up the coals, and add wet wood.

Smoke the swordfish, well covered with the cooker's lid, for 30 to 40 minutes at 190 to 210 degrees F. over a pan of hot water. There will be plenty of time to make the traditional Vietnamese dipping sauce for the fish while the steak is cooking.

Just before serving the swordfish, sprinkle the scallions, cilantro, and basil over it.

VIETNAMESE DIPPING SAUCE

The custom is to serve this accompaniment as a dipping sauce. However, since here the fish to be accented is in steak form, it's perhaps more appropriately served on the side so guests can pour their own to suit their tastes.

MAKES A LITTLE LESS THAN 1 CUP

¼ cup lime juice
2 teaspoons crushed red pepper
3 tablespoons sugar
¼ cup nuoc mam
2 cloves garlic, peeled and put through a garlic press
finely julienned carrots for garnish

Pour the lime juice into a small mixing bowl and add the crushed red pepper. Let the flakes soak in the juice for 10 minutes. Then add the sugar and stir to dissolve. Mix in the *nuoc mam* and garlic. Blend well and pour into a small sauceboat.

Sprinkle the julienned carrots on top just before serving.

GINGERLY SHARK

S hark is a firm-fleshed fish ideal for smoking. Not only is it tender and tasty, but it holds together nicely on the grill — and coming off it — making you appear a master chef.

SERVES 4 TO 6

> 2 to 3 pounds shark steaks about 1 inch thick
> ½ cup (1 stick) butter
> 2 teaspoons dried rosemary, coarsely ground in a
>   mortar and pestle
> 2 tablespoons grated fresh gingerroot
> 2 tablespoons lemon juice

About 1 hour before dinnertime and before preparing the fish for the grill, fire up your smoker so you'll have a good bed of coals ready when you need them.

Crosshatch the shark steaks on both sides with a sharp knife, cutting ¼ inch deep, and lay them out on a large nonreactive platter.

Melt the butter in a small saucepan set over low heat. Add the rosemary, ginger, and lemon juice. Mix well.

Pour half of this buttery sauce over the steaks, turn them, and dribble the remaining sauce over the other side. Let the seasoning permeate the fish for about 15 minutes while your smoker finishes preheating.

Add some soaked wood to the hot coals in your smoker's fire pan and fill the water pan halfway with hot water. Oil the cooking rack lightly, place the shark steaks on the grill, and baste with the sauce left on the platter.

Let the steaks smoke, snugly covered by the cooker's lid, at 190 to 210 degrees F. for 15 to 20 minutes. Then turn them, baste again, and smoke for an additional 15 to 20 minutes. Pour any extra sauce over the shark steaks as they are taken from the grill.

SMOKED BLUEFISH

Bluefish is one of those denizens of the deep that has a lot of flavor — too much, in fact, to suit some folks, although in many cases their taste may have been dictated by sampling mass-marketed bluefish kept overly long in transit, particularly to the interior of the country, and thereby rendered oily and sharp-flavored, perhaps even on the verge of turning. Bluefish really needs to be fresh. The best fillets are from fish you've just caught yourself or been given by a neighbor who brought home more than the family freezer could hold. Fresh fish from a good fishmonger is next best. Supermarket bluefish, well, it can be redeemed from mediocrity by smoking. Many a friend of mine has professed dislike for this particular species only to show, presented with a fillet fresh from the smoker, a sudden boundless appetite for it.

Smoking both highlights and mellows the flavor of bluefish. The moisture rising from the water pan keeps the fish from drying out, yet doesn't permeate it and envelop you in fishy fragrance the way steaming often does. Not too moist, not too dry, just right — that's smoked bluefish.

SERVES 6 TO 8

2 bluefish fillets, 2 to 3 pounds each
½ cup (1 stick) butter
1 tablespoon dried rosemary, coarsely ground in a
    mortar and pestle
1 teaspoon ground white pepper

About 1½ to 2 hours before your fish course, fire up your smoker and start a good bed of coals.

With a fork, perforate a sheet of heavy-duty aluminum foil large enough to fold up around the edges of the bluefish fillets, tray fashion, so that there will be plenty of space for smoke to circulate when they are placed on the grill. Oil the foil lightly, then lay the fillets, skin side down, on it.

Melt the butter in a small saucepan and mix in the rosemary and white pepper. Brush this mixture over the bluefish.

Add some wet wood to the cooker's fire pan and hot water to the water pan, and transfer the fillets on their foil tray to the grill. With the cooker's lid tightly in place, smoke the fish at 210 to 230 degrees F. for 1 to 1½ hours, or until fork tender.

Smoked bluefish is delectable served with a remoulade sauce. This piquant accompaniment can be made up while the fish is cooking.

SIMPLE REMOULADE SAUCE

The fancy version of remoulade sauce is a homemade mayonnaise to which herbs are added in the making. Here the seasoning is simply added to ready-made mayonnaise. The effect is perfectly acceptable.

MAKES A LITTLE MORE THAN 1 CUP

1 cup mayonnaise
½ teaspoon dry mustard
2 tablespoons minced well-drained cucumber pickles
3 tablespoons chopped well-drained capers
2 tablespoons minced fresh parsley
1 teaspoon minced fresh chives
½ teaspoon crushed dried chervil
½ teaspoon crushed dried tarragon

Put a little of the mayonnaise in the bottom of a small mixing bowl and blend in the dry mustard, being sure to press out any lumps with the back of the spoon. Blend in the rest of the mayonnaise, then add the pickles, capers, parsley, chives, chervil, and tarragon. Mix well and transfer to an attractive serving bowl. Cover and chill until needed.

SMOKED GRAVLAX

S moked gravlax probably ranks as a bilingual oxymoron, since in standard culinary parlance both smoking and *grava,* the Swedish term for pickling, are methods of preservation and thus not normally used together. Nevertheless, on the first occasion when, in an experimental mood, I smoked some gravlax, the result was rated delicious by everyone at the table.

Once a delicacy rarely found far from its natural habitat, salmon is becoming a dining staple as fish farms from Norway to Chile raise it in ever-increasing tonnage. It can be expected to dominate the seafood counters of the future. So, as with meatloaf, the more recipes for this fish one has, the better. The following is definitely worth including among them, particularly if you're fond of dill.

SERVES 3 TO 4

> *2 matching 1- to 1½-pound salmon fillets, tail section preferred*
> *⅓ to ½ cup chopped fresh dill*
> *3 tablespoons sugar*
> *2 tablespoons salt*
> *2 teaspoons coarsely ground white pepper*
> *fresh dill sprigs for garnish*

Two days before you plan to serve the smoked gravlax, line a nonreactive ceramic or glass platter slightly larger than the salmon fillets with a piece of heavy-duty aluminum foil big enough to envelop the fish.

Place the chopped dill in a small mixing bowl, sprinkle the sugar, salt, and white pepper over it, and toss lightly but well with a fork.

Sprinkle about one-quarter of this dill mixture along the length of the aluminum foil and lay one piece of salmon, skin side down, on the bed of spices. Cover it with about two-thirds of the remaining dill mixture and place the second fish fillet, skin side up, over the first. Scatter the rest of the seasoning over the second fillet. Wrap the foil around the fillets, folding the edges over to seal them and tucking the ends in securely.

Traditionally, salmon is pressed beneath a weighted board or a heavy dish. I find that an unopened half-gallon juice or milk carton on its side works splendidly and saves refrigerator space, always at a premium when there are teenagers in the house.

Refrigerate the weighted fish for 2 days, turning the packet once or twice a day. How often it's turned isn't as important as that it does get flipped occasionally so both fillets become equally permeated with seasoning.

To smoke the salmon, use any mild hardwood, such as apple or maple — or alder if it's available and you want to add that traditional touch. Bring the temperature of the smoker to 190 to 210 degrees F. and fill the water pan halfway with hot water before placing the salmon fillets side by side, skin side down, on the grill. Make sure the smoker's lid is snugly closed.

The salmon should be nicely done within 45 minutes. However, provided the temperature of the smoker is kept hovering at the lower end of the scale, around 190 degrees F., and the water pan is kept sufficiently filled, the fillets can remain on the grill for several hours without becoming overdone or dry.

Smoked gravlax is best presented as it comes from the grill, the whole fillets regal in their dressing of spices, rather than being thinly sliced in traditional gravlax fashion. A few fresh dill sprigs decorating the dish add attractive contrast and bring out the rich salmon color.

The fillets are sublime served with a Swedish mustard sauce. They are also delicious cold, but rarely can chef or guests be persuaded to wait for them to chill.

SWEDISH MUSTARD SAUCE

In Sweden, sweet mustard is as popular as sharp. Hot dog vendors always carry both, and most customers are very particular about which one they want. When it comes to fish, however, Swedes all seem to agree that the mustard sauce should be sweet.

MAKES ABOUT 1 CUP

> 2 tablespoons prepared mustard
> 1 tablespoon sugar
> 1 tablespoon white vinegar
> 6 tablespoons vegetable oil
> 6 tablespoons sour cream
> 3 tablespoons minced fresh dill

Mix the mustard, sugar, and vinegar in a blender or food processor. Add the oil in a slow stream, combining it well with the other ingredients, then add the sour cream one spoonful at a time, blending after each addition. Lightly stir in all but a bit of the dill.

Transfer the sauce to a small serving bowl and set it out garnished with the reserved dill.

FIG-STUFFED SALMON

Fruit in combination with meat or fish is one of the more distinctive culinary trends of the nineties — or perhaps one should more accurately describe it as a revival, since venison has always been served with currants or wild cranberries, and prunes have accompanied goose and pork since the Middle Ages, when the serving of sweet spices such as cloves and nutmeg with meat came into vogue as well.

Some of the new fruit-accented dishes succeed; others are better on paper than palate. One combination that works particularly well, despite seeming an odd one on first reflection, is that of fresh figs and salmon. Both are mild-flavored and delicate, and they prove highly complementary, particularly when smoked together.

Normally, the tail section of the salmon is preferred over the center. However, there's more room for stuffing in the belly portion, which is why that's your choice for this dish.

SERVES 4 TO 6

2 to 3 pounds salmon, preferably center cut rather than tail
4 fresh figs, sliced
3 tablespoons lime juice
2 tablespoons dark brown sugar
zest of 1 lime

Start a fire in your smoker pan first thing, about 1½ to 2 hours before dinnertime, and build up the coals. Make sure you have a good supply of a mild wood like alder or fruit-fragrant apple soaking in your water bucket. You'll want plenty of aromatic smoke for this dish. You'll also want the temperature in the smoker hovering steadily between 190 and 220 degrees F. and the water in its pan nice and hot when you put the fish on the grill.

Butterfly the salmon. That is, leaving the skin along the back in-

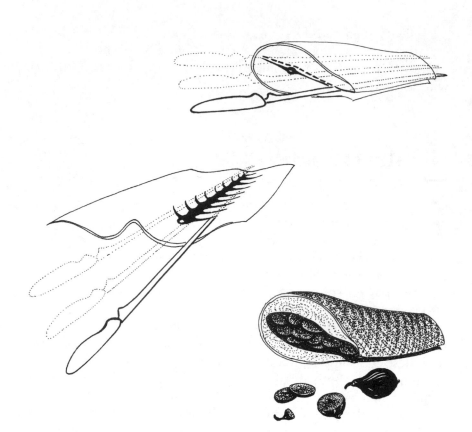

tact to act as a hinge, slice into the fish from the belly side just above the bone, open up the fish, and then work the knife along the underside of the bone until you can remove it. You now effectively have two fish fillets joined on one side.

Place the fig slices in a small mixing bowl and sprinkle them with the lime juice, brown sugar, and lime zest. Toss gently.

Scoop the fig stuffing onto one half of the butterflied salmon. Then fold the second half over the first, enclosing the filling.

Cut a piece of heavy-duty aluminum foil a little longer than the fish and a bit more than twice as wide. Fold it over to form a double thickness of foil. Place the stuffed salmon on the foil and gather the edges up around it a bit to keep the lime juice from dripping out.

Put the fish in its foil boat on the grill and smoke for 1 to 1½ hours at 190 to 220 degrees F. The aroma wafting from under the smoker's lid as the salmon nears perfection will be heavenly.

POTTED SALMON

When it comes to smoke cooking, leftovers seem never to be a problem. In the case of salmon, in fact, I often find I have to toss two pieces of fish on the grill — one for the dinner and one for the leftovers, as it were — if I'm to save any for this dish.

Other smoked fish can be used in this recipe, but the spread is particularly good made with salmon.

MAKES ABOUT 1 QUART

3 cups lightly packed smoked salmon, bones and skin removed
1 cup mayonnaise
½ cup chopped fresh dill
1 tablespoon lemon juice
1 teaspoon prepared mustard
2 to 3 drops Tabasco or similar hot red pepper sauce
¼ cup heavy cream

Flake the fish and place it in a food processor. Add the mayonnaise, dill, lemon juice, mustard, and Tabasco or other hot red pepper sauce. Mix well. Lastly, in a slow stream, drizzle in the cream, blending continuously until smooth.

Transfer the spread to an attractive 1-quart nonreactive ceramic pot, cover tightly, and refrigerate until needed. Kept cold, the potted salmon should last 4 to 5 days.

Serve with crackers, a fresh baguette, or thinly sliced pumpernickel. Some finely chopped sweet onions and capers make splendid help-yourself toppings.

10. ROTI AND KABOBS

By common agreement, the best chicken our family ever tasted was a roti meal in Algeria. Now granted, we'd been driving through the desert for over a month, were low on supplies, and hadn't seen fresh meat in all that time, which no doubt had something to do with our verdict. So, no doubt, had the fact that the local fowl were truly range fed, literally scratching for a living in the wilderness. But the masterstroke was the spit roasting.

Roti, or rotisserie cooking, probably originated with early nomadic tribes. Someone roasting chunks of meat on a stick noticed that turning the stick slowly resulted in more evenly broiled morsels. The simple technique endured, little changed, for thousands of years, the sticks growing and shrinking in size. In medieval banquet halls, whole oxen were roasted on huge spits, and in countless villages throughout the Orient and the Middle East, bite-size morsels of fish, fowl, and mutton were threaded onto small skewers for grilling.

There's something very appealing — playful, even — about skewer cooking. In the kitchens of Morocco and elsewhere throughout the Middle and Far East, small charcoal braziers are found to this day, often right next to the food processor. Moving into an era of personal computers and satellite dishes, modern householders will still not give up their kabobs.

In this country, thanks to the retro nineties, both roti and kabobs, largely absent from the culinary scene for a while, are making a big comeback. This time around, the difference is smoke. Charcoal-fired smokers such as the Swisher come with a rotisserie attachment as part of the package, and gas-fired grills like the Sterling and the Duncane are often also equipped for rotisserie cooking.

One can argue that the indirect heat of smoking renders a rotisserie unnecessary. Smoke cookers circulate the heat, not the meat, as someone once epigrammatically, and quite correctly, put it. All the same, a rotating spit causes the natural juices and fat of a cut of meat to roll around its outer surface as it revolves. This natural basting laps up the smoke and moisture wafting from the nether reaches of the cooker and wraps them around the roasting meat.

The trick to successful self-basting here lies in ensuring that nowhere does the meat protrude beyond the perimeter of the water pan beneath it. You want to maximize the flavor recirculating around whatever's cooking without exposing the meat to the drying effect of direct heat or letting the fat drip into the fire instead of the water pan, causing flare-ups.

A more cogent argument against rotisseries has to do with the matter of balance. By power-driven spit as by hand, albeit less discernibly, turning a large piece of meat for a long time is quite a job. Turning a large piece of meat that's out of balance for a long time is beyond the capacity of many rotisserie motors. This is why so many rotisseries sit unused after the first couple of tries.

A vertical spit, often used in commercial gyro cookers, is one — quite upstanding, if you'll pardon the pun — solution to this problem. Another is to make certain that any large cut of meat is both properly balanced when first positioned on the spit and firmly secured at either end by the prongs. For like reasons, the legs and wings of fowl should be lashed down where the prongs are not long enough to truss them.

That said, let me add that spit roasting lends an indefinable touch of culinary genius to the cooking of, say, a whole fowl or a leg of lamb — or gyros, which by very definition are turned. The rotisserie can move a meal from fine to fabulous. Its smaller cousin, the kabob, ideal for smaller morsels like seafood, makes a meal just plain relaxing fun.

COMBINATION GYROS

A gyro — the name derives from the Greek word for "circle" or "rounded" — can't be cooked on something other than a rotating spit, any more than a roller coaster can be designed without the swoops. Traditionally, gyros are associated with lamb. Here the combination of lamb and beef lends contrast to the dish. When you add the wet wood to your smoker's fire pan, toss in some freshly cut sage from the garden as well for a distinctive herbal flavor and a cooking fragrance that will drive you positively wild waiting.

SERVES 8 TO 10

1 boneless leg of lamb, about 3 pounds
2- to 3-pound boneless beef round steak
¼ cup crushed dried oregano
¼ cup crushed dried basil
6 cloves garlic, peeled and slivered
1 teaspoon ground thyme
1 teaspoon ground sage
1 teaspoon ground black pepper
1 teaspoon salt
olive oil

Start a fire in your rotisserie first thing, about 5 to 7 hours before your gyro repast, to build up a good bed of coals, and make sure you have an ample supply of wood soaking.

Set the leg of lamb and the round steak out on a large cutting board or butcher block and pound both cuts energetically with a meat mallet. While your efforts will help to tenderize the meat, your main purpose is to shape the pieces. You want to coax each of them into a rectangular form measuring some 10 to 12 inches by 12 to 14 inches.

Lay several 2-foot lengths of untreated cotton cord about 1 to 2 inches apart on your working surface and place the flattened lamb lengthwise over them. Then turn your attention to the seasoning.

In a small mixing bowl, stir together the oregano, basil, slivered garlic, thyme, sage, pepper, and salt.

Brush the top of the lamb with olive oil, then sprinkle about one-third of the herb mixture over it. Pound the meat again to press the seasoning into the lamb.

Lay the steak on top of the lamb, brush the beef with more olive oil, and sprinkle it with another one-third of the seasoning, again pressing it into the meat. Reserve the remaining herbs.

The next step may take an extra pair of hands. Roll up the sandwiched lamb and beef the long way, coiling them as tightly as you can. Tie the roll fast with the cotton cords.

Insert the rotisserie spit through the core of the combination roast and slide the prongs firmly into place. Then, just before positioning the spit in your smoker, brush the rolled roast once more with olive oil and pat the remaining herbs into it, working the seasoning in all around the outside.

Close the rotisserie lid and smoke the roast at 210 to 230 degrees F. over hot water and soaked wood or chips for 4 to 6 hours, depending on how rare or well-done you like your meat. When the gyro is nearly done to your liking, add some sprigs of garden sage, including the stems, to the fire pan for a final herby accent.

To serve, take the roast from the spit and let it sit for 10 to 15 minutes before carving. Gyros are traditionally sliced very thin.

ROTI LEG OF LAMB

L eg of lamb is a lovely barbecue dish, ever popular, although for me no occasion on which it's been served has ever matched the first. Sue and I and a couple of friends, Geoff and Marie Bullock, were camped by Forked Lake in the Adirondacks when one day we were seized by an irrepressible desire for some real food instead of the foil-packed dehydrated meals we'd been toting around. A tin-plate serving of macaroni and cheese takes you only so far. We snuck into town and procured a whole leg of lamb to spit-roast, along with some celebratory wine.

No sooner had we returned to camp than it began to rain. Rain, in the form of a perpetual cold drizzle making it difficult to discern where the air ends and a lake begins, is not an unusual commodity on Adirondack waterways.

Did we but know it, the rain was to continue for the duration of our stay. That evening, the lamb seemed destined to take almost as long to roast. The fire smoldered and smoked. The lamb, on its sagging wooden spit, hugged the coals for warmth. We waited, and we waited, and we waited. The bread was gone by nine o'clock, the second bottle of wine by ten. The sluggish fire did nothing to keep us warm and very little to advance the cooking of the lamb.

By ten-thirty, we could stand it no longer. We sliced off servings of rare meat from all along the joint. It was succulent, smoky, and delicious.

The following recipe calls for a boned leg of lamb because that's more easily balanced on a rotisserie spit than the bone-in version used that evening. Squatting by the smoker in a steady drizzle is optional.

SERVES 8 TO 10

3- to 5-pound boneless leg of lamb, whole or butterflied
1 small whole bulb garlic, the cloves peeled and halved
1 large fresh rosemary sprig

THE GLAZE

½ cup firmly packed dark brown sugar
½ cup currant jelly
¼ cup cider vinegar
1 teaspoon ground nutmeg
1 teaspoon ground black pepper

About 5½ to 6½ hours before your planned lamb dinner, fire up your rotisserie and start a good bed of coals. Then turn to the lamb preparations.

If what you have is a butterflied joint, it will need to be tied into a snug roll. A regular whole boned leg of lamb may still require tying depending on how the boning was done. What you want to prevent is any slack or slippage while the meat is rotating. Use untreated cotton cord or cotton sheeting strips for any tying you need to do.

With a sharp, thin knife, make a series of incisions spaced about 1 inch apart all around the meat. Slip half a garlic clove and a rosemary leaf into each slit as you make it.

Slide the seasoned joint onto the rotisserie spit, checking that it's well balanced before anchoring it in place with the prongs. Let rest while you put together a glaze for it.

Measure the brown sugar, currant jelly, vinegar, nutmeg, and pepper into a small stainless steel or flameproof ceramic saucepan and whisk while heating to a simmer. When the mixture is smooth, remove from the heat.

Add wet wood or chips to your rotisserie's fire pan and set a pan of hot water in place. Then put the spit in place and brush the lamb lightly with the glazing mixture. Smoke, covered, at 210 to 230 degrees F. for 5 to 6 hours, glazing every 30 minutes or so.

If you don't have a rotisserie attachment for your cooker, the lamb can be smoked on a regular grill provided you rotate it one-quarter of a turn every 30 minutes and brush the new upper surface well with the glaze.

BACON-BARDED CHICKEN

R ecipes, whether family ones or haute cuisine, tend to become more complex with use. Maybe just a hint of cilantro is added here, a touch of cinnamon there. A few mushrooms enhance a dish one day and become part and parcel of the recipe. Some medieval recipes are known to have listed 30 to 40 separate ingredients, and classic French cuisine was noted for its ornate sauces and time-consuming side preparations. The sauce chef became a master in his own right, his domain a separate culinary jurisdiction.

Yet the fact is that sometimes simple is outstanding, as French chefs will also acknowledge. Take, for instance, this modest chicken dish.

Barding, originally denoting the armoring of a horse, in culinary terms refers to wrapping meats in fat. Devised to protect fragile or lean cuts such as venison roasts from drying out, it also does wonders for the taste of chicken.

SERVES 2 TO 4

2- to 3-pound fryer
1 clove garlic, mashed flat at one end
1 lemon, quartered
1 small bunch fresh parsley
1 small bunch fresh sage
1 small bunch fresh rosemary
6 thick strips bacon

Start the fire in your rotisserie some 2 hours or so before this dish is to be served and before starting the other preparations for it.

Rinse the chicken briefly under running water, drain, and pat dry with a paper towel. Rub the bird inside and out with the mashed end of the garlic.

Squeeze the juice from the lemon quarters into the chicken cavity, then drop in the spent wedges. Add the parsley, sage, and rosemary, alternating the sprigs. Theoretically, the opening should be sewn or skewered closed. Myself, I simply put the chicken on the spit, overlap the skin, and secure with the prongs.

The shortcut isn't always completely successful. Sometimes, halfway through the cooking of the bird, part of the seasoning spills out because the skin has shrunk. The loss is usually confined to a few herb sprigs and a lemon wedge or two, however, and by that time they've already imparted most of their flavor to the chicken. Besides, they only fall into the water pan, where their fragrance, wafting upward with the moisture, continues to accent the cooking.

Shortcut or no, once the dressed chicken has been secured, wrap the bacon strips around it, pinning them down with poultry-lacing skewers at the ends and the middle or tying them on with untreated cotton cord. This is not bona fide barding, which historically calls for sheets of fat, at best difficult to find these days. The flavor it adds, though, is fantastic.

While I may be cavalier about lacing up the chicken cavity in this instance, I do make sure I truss the bacon-wrapped bird, again using untreated cotton cord, to keep the legs from flopping or even breaking free if the fowl is for some reason left to smoke longer than originally planned. There's little danger of overcooking or drying out fowl that's being smoked, but it can become so tender that, revolving on a rotisserie spit, it quite literally falls apart.

Add some wet wood or chips to your coals, put a pan of hot water in place, and smoke the chicken at 220 to 240 degrees F., keeping the rotisserie tightly closed, for 1½ to 2 hours, or until done, when the juice will run clear if the inner side of a thigh is pierced with a fork. Don't forget to pull out the poultry skewers or remove the string before serving.

PERSIAN STUFFED CHICKEN

While it may be politically incorrect to refer to this dish as Persian rather than Iranian these days, the blend of fruits and spices creating its distinctive flavor predates the centuries of social strife leading eventually to the change in terminology on the geopolitical front. The recipe is loosely based on a meal my wife and I were served in the sixties at a small restaurant in Tehran down the street from the Amir Kabir, a hippie hotel above a used-tire shop known far and wide for its washing facilities, notably scarce in that region in those days.

Between the hotel and the restaurant was situated a vendor of fresh pomegranate juice, an absolutely unbelievable delight in the desert heat of the area. We stopped for juice both coming and going and afterward felt as if we had wined and dined with the emperor himself in Persepolis.

SERVES 4 TO 6

3½- to 4½-pound roasting chicken
⅓ cup butter, divided
1 medium-size onion, finely chopped
20 seedless green grapes
10 dried apricots, chopped
6 prunes, pitted and chopped
½ cup blanched almonds, chopped
½ cup pine nuts
¼ cup dried currants
1 teaspoon ground allspice
½ teaspoon ground cinnamon
½ teaspoon crushed dried tarragon
½ teaspoon ground black pepper
½ teaspoon salt

Start building up a good bed of coals in your rotisserie about 5½ to 6½ hours before you plan to serve this dish. Then turn to the preparations for the fowl.

Rinse the chicken briefly under running water, drain, and pat dry with a paper towel. Set aside while you prepare the stuffing.

In a fairly large frying pan, melt half the butter, about 3 tablespoonfuls, over low heat. Add the onion and sauté until soft and translucent. Then add the remainder of the butter, let melt, and stir in the grapes, apricots, and prunes, separating the sticky pieces if need be as you stir. Add the almonds, pine nuts, and currants. Sauté for 2 to 3 minutes to plump the fruit and coat the nuts with butter.

Remove the pan from the heat and stir in the allspice, cinnamon, tarragon, pepper, and salt, blending well.

Allow the seasoned stuffing to cool until it can be easily handled. Then fill the chicken cavity loosely with the mixture. Pin the opening closed with poultry-lacing skewers.

Center the chicken on the rotisserie spit, balancing it well, and slide the prongs into place, anchoring the fowl securely. Tying the legs together with untreated cotton cord will prevent their loosening or even breaking free as the bird reaches the falling-apart stage of succulent doneness.

Add wet wood or chips to the coals in the rotisserie, set a pan of hot water in place, close the cooker, and smoke the chicken for 5 to 6 hours at 210 to 230 degrees F., replenishing the supplies of wood and water as needed. The chicken will be done once the juice runs clear when you insert a fork into the inner side of a thigh, but give it another 30 minutes on the spit for the benefit of the stuffing.

If you don't have a rotisserie attachment for your cooker, the chicken can be smoked on a regular grill provided you rotate it one-quarter of a turn every 30 minutes.

However it's cooked, it's hard to say which is tastier here, the rich stuffing or the bird.

PHILIPPINE CHICKEN

T he Philippine culture has always been one of the most assimilat-
ing in the Far East. The amalgam stretches way back to include
Spanish influences absorbed over four hundred years of colonial
rule.

These influences are particularly apparent in the culinary fare of
the Philippines, frequented by such island-alien ingredients as Iberian chorizos, raisins, and olives. The Philippine stuffed rolled beef
morcon is such a dish. Essentially the same stuffing is used in this
chicken recipe.

SERVES 6 TO 8

6- to 7-pound roasting chicken

THE MARINADE AND BASTE
½ cup soy sauce
½ cup lemon juice
6 cloves garlic, peeled and put through a garlic press
2 teaspoons ground black pepper
1 teaspoon salt

THE STUFFING
2 medium-size carrots, cut into 1-inch lengths
2 cups diced cooked ham
2 cups finely sliced cooked chorizo sausages
¼ cup raisins
20 small pimento-stuffed green olives
4 gherkins, each sliced into 4 to 6 pieces
2 hard-boiled eggs, peeled

About 5½ to 6½ hours before dinnertime, start a fire in your rotisserie and add a good supply of coals to heat.

Rinse the chicken, pat dry with a paper towel, and let rest on a
nonreactive platter or dish with a good rim while you prepare a
quick marinade.

In a small mixing bowl, combine the soy sauce, lemon juice, garlic, pepper, and salt. Brush some of this mixture onto the chicken,
reserving the remainder.

Parboil the carrot sections for 3 minutes in a small saucepan. Drain well and let cool.

Meanwhile, in a medium-size mixing bowl, gently toss together the ham, chorizos, raisins, olives, and gherkin pieces.

Put about one-third of this stuffing into the chicken cavity. Place one of the eggs on top of the stuffing and cover it with half of the carrot pieces. Then add another one-third of the stuffing, the second egg, and the remainder of the carrots. Finish with the last one-third of the stuffing. Pin the chicken cavity closed with poultry-lacing skewers and tie the legs together snugly with untreated cotton cord.

Add some wet wood or chips to your rotisserie and fill the water pan halfway with hot water. Spear the chicken with the rotisserie rod, anchor the bird with the prongs so that it is well balanced, and position the spit in the smoker.

Smoke the stuffed chicken at 210 to 230 degrees F. for 5 to 6 hours, or until done, when the juice will run clear from a pierced inner thigh. Baste every 45 minutes to 1 hour with the remaining marinade sauce, checking the fuel, smoke wood, and water while you're at it.

In the original *morcon,* the eggs are sliced as you slice the meat. Here, when you dish out the stuffing, cut and divide the eggs among the servings.

MARMALADE-GLAZED DUCK

W hen I was a kid," goes a family lecture of mine, "we had two jars of jam open at the same time, orange marmalade and raspberry, or maybe apricot. Look at this mess!" I pull half a dozen jars of preserves from the very back of the bottommost shelf of the refrigerator, all with just two or three spoonfuls of their contents left inside. "Why doesn't anybody ever finish one jar before opening another one?"

Refrigerators are that way, though. The back bottom shelf breeds small smidgen-filled containers. When I've rounded up a bunch of jelly and jam ones, we have smoked duck.

Any combination of flavors will serve the purpose here. The ones mentioned in the recipe just happened to be the bottom-shelf residents the last time I smoked a duck. You don't need three different varieties, either. You can use two or six or whatever, although a bit of marmalade is awfully nice to have among them. What you do need is a full cup's worth of smidgens.

Another thing you don't absolutely need for this recipe is a rotisserie. The rotating spit just makes things easier, that's all. Provided you turn and baste the duck a couple of times during the smoking process so that it's glazed all over at least twice, an ordinary smoker will do the job quite capably.

The recipe given here is a modification of a standard Chinese method of cooking duck that results in a moist but not fatty bird. It doesn't take much preparation time. However, a fair amount of time — the better part of a day, actually — is needed for the duck to dry properly.

SERVES 2 TO 4 DEPENDING ON THE SIZE OF THE DUCK

4- to 6-pound duck
1 lemon, quartered

THE GLAZE

½ cup honey
½ cup orange marmalade
¼ cup cherry jam
¼ cup apricot jam
¼ cup lemon juice
2 tablespoons grated fresh gingerroot
1 teaspoon Tabasco or similar hot red pepper sauce

First thing in the morning on the day of your duck dinner, put a big pot of water on to boil.

While it's heating, turn your attention to the bird. Pull or cut off any extra chunks of fat left around the neck and tail, then rinse the duck inside and out under running water and pat dry with a paper towel. Prick the skin all over with a sharp fork — lightly, though, so you don't jab the meat too much. Tie the legs together loosely with strong untreated cotton cord.

When the water has come to a boil, add the lemon quarters to the pot and slowly lower the duck into the hot liquid. Let simmer for 10 minutes.

Fish the bird out by the string — a chopstick is handy here — and let it drain briefly on end in a colander, making sure the neck skin isn't folded over itself, trapping water inside the fowl.

Once it's stopped dripping, hang the duck in a well-ventilated spot to dry for 3 to 4 hours, or longer if that happens to be more convenient. Outside is the best place for it, provided you avoid direct sunlight, and I've hung ducks on everything from a tree branch to a clothesline to a hook on a screened porch during fly season, but over the sink is fine, too, if you have something there to hang it from.

About 4½ to 5½ hours before dinnertime, start preheating your rotisserie. While the coals are settling down for a good long smoke, prepare the glazing sauce for the duck.

In a small stainless steel or ceramic saucepan, mix the honey, marmalade, and cherry and apricot jams — or 1 cupful of whatever other varieties you happen to have on hand. If the preserves are chunky, whirl them in a blender or food processor first to reduce large pieces of fruit to small ones.

Add the lemon juice, ginger, and Tabasco or other hot red pepper sauce to the jam in the pan and mix well. Bring the mixture to a boil, then simmer over low heat for 5 to 10 minutes, or until the sauce is quite thick. Set aside.

Put some wet wood or chips in the rotisserie's fire pan, set a pan of hot water in place, and position the duck on the spit, balancing it well so that it will rotate easily.

Close the cover of the rotisserie and smoke the duck at 210 to 230 degrees F. for 30 minutes. After this initial smoking period, brush the fruit glaze over the rotating duck.

Continue to smoke the duck for 3½ to 4½ more hours, glazing it again with the syrupy fruit every 30 minutes or so until all the sauce is used up.

The skin of this bird may not be crispy, but it won't be fatty either, and the roti duck beneath will be succulent and juicy indeed.

TURKEY KABOBS

Kabobs, the mini version of roti, evoke an even broader range of possibilities than those suggested by their larger counterpart. Experimentation is definitely in order here. It's part of the fun of skewer cooking. For a start, however, try this method of preparing turkey morsels, which transforms them from the somewhat ordinary to the opulent.

All too often turkey has lost both its succulence and its savor by the time it reaches the table. This is particularly true where solitary mouthfuls of it are involved, as in kabobs, and since nowadays turkey derives its appeal in part from its status as healthy low-fat fare, the old trick of wrapping the tidbits in bacon is frowned upon.

Just between you and me, the bacon wrap is still a very tasty way to prepare shish kebabs. Be that as it may, here's another technique to keep bite-size morsels of turkey juicy and flavorsome. The secret lies in the moisturizing olive oil baste and the fragrant, sheltering sun-dried tomatoes.

SERVES 4 TO 6

2 pounds turkey breast, cut into 1½-inch cubes
½ cup lemon juice
½ cup honey
¼ cup olive oil
2 teaspoons crushed dried oregano
1 teaspoon ground sage
1 teaspoon ground white pepper
½ teaspoon salt
8 ounces sun-dried tomatoes packed in olive oil

The day before the kabobs are to be served, set out a nonreactive mixing bowl large enough to accommodate the turkey pieces along with a marinade.

Measure into the bowl the lemon juice, honey, olive oil, oregano, sage, white pepper, and salt — while most smoke cooking doesn't need salt, you might want a pinch here. Whisk until well blended.

Add the turkey cubes and turn them in the liquid to distribute the marinade well. Let the turkey steep, tightly covered and refrigerated, overnight.

The following day, start a fire in your smoker about 2½ hours before you want to serve the kabobs. While the coals are settling, prepare the skewers.

Thread the marinated turkey cubes and sun-dried tomatoes alternately onto the skewers, pressing the pieces together so they're quite snug. This helps to hold the soft tomatoes in place. Reserve the marinade for basting.

Add wet smoking wood to your fire pan and hot water to the water pan. Then arrange the skewers on the grill and baste liberally with some of the leftover marinade.

Put the lid on the cooker and smoke the kabobs at 210 to 230 degrees F. for about 45 minutes, then turn and baste them with more of the marinade. Smoke for another 45 minutes, baste once more, and cover again for a final 30 minutes of smoking. Just before taking them from the grill, give them a finishing baste.

SHRIMP AND ASPARAGUS EN BROCHETTE

A mong the shellfish, shrimp lend themselves naturally to shish kebabs, coming as they do in bite-size pieces. The little crustaceans and asparagus are a natural team, their contrasting colors and textures adding a special dimension to the distinctive flavor of each. They are also both delicacies associated with luxury over the years, although today shrimp is everywhere at very reasonable prices, and so is asparagus when it's in season.

A certain mystique surrounds the proper preparation and cooking of asparagus in classic European cuisine. In my youth, the spears were steamed until soft, artfully embellished, presented on a special elongated asparagus platter, and served with broad, flat, ornately engraved silver asparagus tongs. Today these exotic utensils are displayed in the china cabinet, and the contemporary palate prefers practically everything al dente, including this vegetable. Asparagus is served almost crisp — and, in our family, exceedingly often during April and May, when our asparagus patch is yielding its best.

As it happens, the height of the asparagus harvest coincides with the time when I usually haul the smokers out of hibernation for another season of billowing smoke. Since the bounty lingers into May, it overlaps our honey harvest as well. So here's a recipe that combines the fruits of all those spring endeavors.

SERVES 6 TO 8 AS AN APPETIZER, 3 TO 4 AS AN ENTRÉE

2 pounds (32 to 40) shrimp in the shell
½ cup lime juice
½ cup honey
¼ cup olive oil
2 tablespoons soy sauce
16 medium-thick stalks asparagus
4 tablespoons butter

The day before you plan to serve this dish, peel the shrimp and set aside while you prepare the marinade.

Pour the lime juice, honey, olive oil, and soy sauce into a large mixing bowl suitable for marinating. Stir to blend.

Add the shrimp and turn in the marinade until well coated, then cover tightly with plastic wrap and let steep, refrigerated, overnight.

About 2 hours before dinnertime on the following day, wash the asparagus and snap or cut off the tough bottom ends. Cut the remaining stalks into thirds.

Fire up the smoker and start a bed of coals. While the cooker is heating, thread the shrimp and asparagus pieces alternately onto bamboo skewers. Reserve the marinade.

Let the skewers rest until the smoker reaches 200 to 230 degrees F. Meanwhile, melt the butter in a small nonreactive saucepan and add the reserved marinade. Bring to a boil, lower the heat, and simmer for 5 minutes.

Add wet wood to the smoker's fire pan and set a pan of hot water in place. Arrange the skewers on the grill, baste with the heated marinade, and tightly cover the smoker.

Continue basting the skewers every 10 minutes until the shrimp and asparagus are done to your taste, which at 200 to 230 degrees F. will take about 30 minutes. The shrimp should be pink but still slightly translucent.

SKEWERED SCALLOPS

In our vegetable garden, basil and cherry tomatoes are almost as plentiful as the squashes. As long as we keep pinching the buds off the basil before it blooms, it sends out new greenery all summer long. As for the cherry tomatoes, especially the newer varieties like the Sweet 100s, come August they simply overflow their racemes, the tiny bright red fruits cascading everywhere about the plants.

Throughout those summery harvest days, both the basil and the tomatoes grace our supper table often. They are also much eaten out of hand during the tending of the garden. However, their sheer abundance prompts a constant search for more ways in which to utilize them in their natural combination, which is how this dish evolved.

SERVES 4 TO 6 AS AN APPETIZER, 2 AS AN ENTRÉE

1 pound (about 2 dozen) sea scallops
¼ cup sweet vermouth
2 teaspoons dark brown sugar
½ teaspoon ground white pepper
¼ teaspoon ground nutmeg
20 to 25 cherry tomatoes
40 to 50 fresh basil leaves, stemmed
4 tablespoons butter

About 1 hour before you plan to serve the skewered scallops, fire up your smoker and start a good bed of coals going.

Next, drain the scallops and pat dry with a paper towel.

In a medium-size mixing bowl, combine the sweet vermouth, brown sugar, white pepper, and nutmeg. Blend well. Add the scallops and set aside to marinate at room temperature for 30 minutes.

To prepare for smoking, thread the scallops onto bamboo skewers, interspersing a cherry tomato with a basil leaf on either side of each scallop. Reserve the marinade.

Melt the butter in a small saucepan set over low heat, add the reserved marinade, and bring to a simmer before removing from the stove.

Add some wet wood to your smoker's fire pan and hot water to the water pan, then place the skewers on the grill. Baste with the butter and marinade mixture before covering the cooker.

Smoke the scallops at 190 to 210 degrees F. for 10 minutes, then turn and baste the skewered morsels again. Smoke for another 5 to 10 minutes or until the scallops have turned opaque and are just cooked through. Baste one last time before taking the skewers from the grill.

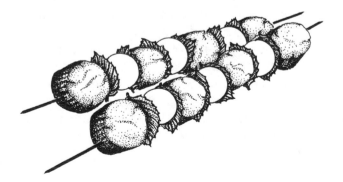

SKEWERED OCTOPUS

O ctopus is one of those dishes that inspire a definite response. Either you relish it or you shudder at the very thought of it. That said, I quite fancy octopus myself, although Susan would much rather dine on something else. My fondness for the dish no doubt stems in part from memories of quiet waterfront repasts in the charming medieval Slovenian town of Piran. There, grilled octopus is as common as the sunshine suffusing the Mediterranean, seen from the terraced cafés.

By virtue of its very constitution, octopus is mostly a chewy conveyor of sauce. Pounding octopods for an hour or so will tenderize them to an extent. But that exercise rather defeats the purpose of eating octopus in the first place. With the cephalopod, as with jerky, chewiness is the essence. To attribute softness to either one would be an oxymoron.

SERVES 6 TO 8 AS AN APPETIZER, 2 TO 4 AS AN ENTRÉE

1½-pound octopus
½ cup white wine
⅓ cup olive oil
6 cloves garlic, peeled and put through a garlic press
1 tablespoon crushed red pepper
4 tablespoons chopped fresh parsley
salt to taste

The day before you want to serve these kabobs, rinse the octopus and lay it on a large cutting board or butcher block. First cut off the tentacles. For this I use a large Chinese kitchen knife, the kind that looks like a meat cleaver. This is a great tool for difficult food cutting provided one remembers to use it with a knifelike cutting motion rather than swinging it like a cleaver. A large, sharp kitchen knife will also do the trick, but it doesn't have behind it the weight that allows the Chinese knife to make tough cuts so easily.

Split the octopus body in half from tentacles to top. Cut out and discard the inner organs, beak, and eyes. Rinse the octopus and pat dry. Then cut the tentacles and body sections into 1-inch pieces.

Place the octopus in a medium-size bowl or pan suitable for marinating and set aside.

In a small stainless steel or flameproof ceramic saucepan, mix together the wine, olive oil, garlic, and crushed red pepper. Simmer over low heat for 5 minutes. Let cool, then add the parsley.

Pour the liquid over the octopus and stir to coat the pieces well. Marinate overnight, covered and refrigerated. Don't expect the marinade to penetrate the octopus deeply, though.

The following day, about 2½ hours before dinnertime, fire up your smoker and start a good bed of coals. While the cooker is heating, drain and thread the octopus sections on bamboo skewers, reserving the marinade.

Smoke the kabobs in a well-covered cooker at 200 to 220 degrees F. for 2 hours over a combination of coals and wet wood and a pan of hot water.

Just before serving, heat the reserved marinade to the boiling point in a small saucepan, reduce the heat, and simmer for 5 minutes.

Lay the octopus kabobs on their serving platter, salt lightly, and douse with the hot marinade.

ZESTY SWORDFISH KABOBS

S wordfish, which lends itself admirably to smoke cooking because of its distinct, robust flavor, is also a seafood particularly suited to kabobs, holding together well as it cooks. When you're threading cubes of swordfish steak onto a skewer, insert the stick crosswise to the whorls. So anchored, the squares will be quite secure.

SERVES 4

1½ to 2 pounds swordfish steak
½ cup olive oil
½ cup lemon juice
1 tablespoon lemon zest
1 teaspoon ground cayenne pepper
1 teaspoon ground white pepper
½ teaspoon salt

The day before the swordfish kabobs are to be smoked, cut the fish into 1- to 1½-inch cubes. Set aside while you make the marinade.

In a fairly large mixing bowl suitable for marinating, combine the olive oil, lemon juice and zest, cayenne and white peppers, and salt. Blend well.

Add the swordfish cubes to the bowl and gently turn the pieces in the marinade to make sure they're covered on all sides with the liquid. Refrigerate, closely covered, overnight. In the morning, turn the swordfish pieces in their marinade again.

About 1½ hours before you plan to serve the kabobs, take the swordfish from the refrigerator to finish marinating at room temperature while you fire up the smoker and start the coals heating.

Then thread the fish cubes onto wooden skewers, reserving the marinade.

Add wet wood to your smoker's fire pan, fill the water pan partway with hot water, place the skewers on the grill, and cover the smoker tightly.

Smoke the swordfish at 190 to 220 degrees F. for about 45 minutes, turning the skewers over and basting the fish with marinade after the first 20 minutes or so. Brush again with marinade just before taking the swordfish from the grill.

KIDNEY KABOBS

The term *variety meats* covers a broad range of fare, from lights to sweetbreads, not all that popular in this country. Now I, uncharacteristically for a child, honestly enjoyed liver as a kid, while a good dish of kidneys, well, that could transport me to seventh heaven. Then, in college, I discovered James Joyce's line in *Ulysses,* "Leopold Bloom ate with relish the inner organs of beasts and fowls," and pronounced it a classic passage. So it probably goes without saying that I was bound to include in this volume at least one recipe for kidneys. If you are less than fond of them, I trust you'll feel free to simply skip the rest of this particular entry, remembering as you do so that a few of us out there quite fancy this dish and should probably thank you for helping not to elevate it to the status of a high-priced delicacy.

SERVES 4

> 16 lamb kidneys, about 1½ to 2 pounds
> 16 pearl onions
> ½ cup (1 stick) butter
> 2 teaspoons dried rosemary, crushed
> 1 teaspoon ground white pepper
> ½ teaspoon ground nutmeg

About 1½ to 2 hours before you plan to serve the kidneys, start a fire in the smoker and add coals to start heating. Then turn your attention to the kidneys.

Remove any membranes and outer fat from the kidneys, then slice into the center of each one far enough to cut out the white core. Try to keep the cut small, though. Rinse the kidneys briefly under running water and pat dry with a paper towel. Set aside for the moment.

Put a small saucepan of water on to heat. Peel the onions, and when the water has reached a rolling boil, drop them in. Simmer gently until almost done but still firm. About 10 minutes should do it. Drain well.

When the onions are cool enough to handle, thread them and the kidneys alternately onto bamboo skewers.

Melt the butter in the saucepan and add the rosemary, white pepper, and nutmeg. Keep warm while you add wet wood to your smoker's fire pan and hot water to the water pan. Then brush the seasoned butter on the kidneys and onions, coating them on all sides, and place the skewers on the grill.

Smoke the kidneys and onions for 1 to 1½ hours at 210 to 230 degrees F., removing the cover from the grill only to baste the skewers every 30 minutes. Give them one last light baste just before serving.

ANTICUCHOS

A favorite street snack in Peru, *anticuchos* are the counterpart of our hot dogs. The skewered tidbits are spicy and flavorful — and, well, substantial. "So what do you think?" I asked on serving a homemade version to my family.

Our daughter Tanya seemed to consider her response. "It's great, really tender. Dare I ask what it is?"

"Let's just say it's Peru's second-favorite snack — after broiled guinea pig."

"I was afraid of something like that." She kept right on eating, however.

Anticuchos are in fact bite-size morsels of beef heart. Chunks of sirloin can be substituted for them, but do try the original recipe. The authentic *anticuchos* really are delicious.

You'll find both the reddish achiote, or annatto seeds, and anchos, or dried poblano chilies, in the Latin American section of your supermarket.

SERVES 4 TO 6

2- to 3-pound beef heart, white outer wall trimmed, cut into
  1-inch cubes (or a like quantity of sirloin, cubed)
1 cup white vinegar
2 tablespoons olive oil
3 fresh jalapeños or other hot green peppers, stemmed, seeded,
  and chopped
2 anchos, stemmed, seeded, and chopped
4 cloves garlic, peeled
2 teaspoons achiote
1 teaspoon ground cumin
1 teaspoon ground black pepper
½ teaspoon salt

The day before you'd like to serve *anticuchos,* place the cubed meat in a fairly large nonreactive glass or ceramic dish and let rest while you prepare the marinade.

Pour the vinegar into a blender or food processor and add the olive oil, jalapeños or other hot green peppers, anchos, and garlic. Measure in the achiote, cumin, pepper, and salt. Blend the ingredients to a smooth puree.

Pour the marinade over the meat and with a spoon — this marinade is peppery enough to really sting if it gets into even tiny cuts on your hands — turn the pieces in the bowl to make sure each is well coated on all sides with the marinade. Refrigerate the meat, tightly covered, overnight.

The following day, fire up your smoker about 2½ hours before you'd like the *anticuchos* to be ready. Thread the cubes of beef heart — using a fork, not your hands, remember — onto bamboo skewers. Reserve the extra marinade for basting.

Add some wet wood to the coals in your smoker and fill the water pan halfway with hot water. Then lay the skewers of meat crosswise on the grill.

Smoke the *anticuchos* at 200 to 230 degrees F. for 2 hours, turning and basting them every 30 minutes. Work quickly so that the smoker doesn't lose too much heat during these intervals when the lid is off.

CHICKEN HEARTS AND LIVERS SATAY

The cultural definition of food to a large extent dictates what we eat and what we don't. On the East Coast and particularly in the New York area, for instance, chicken livers are consumed in considerable quantities, while the populace in other areas of the country often look askance at this predilection. Now chicken hearts, on the other hand, have become popular at New York meat counters only since the influx of Spanish-speaking people to the city. Both specialty items come from the same fowl, yet most folks eat one or the other or neither.

Here's a dish that not only combines the two determinedly separate traditions but links them with a third, the satay cuisine of the Far East. Satay refers to skewered meat as it's served from the Malay Peninsula to the Indonesian archipelago. There every country, not to mention every village, seems to have its own recipe for this delicacy.

The most common accompaniment is a peanut sauce, again in a thousand variants, but *sambal kecap,* a chili dip, is often seen as well. Recipes for both are included here so that you can take your pick or mix and match.

The tamarind the two recipes call for can be found on the shelves of Asian groceries, sometimes as a paste, sometimes in the form of *canh chua me,* a tamarind soup base flavored with onion, shrimp powder, and other complementary spices. Fresh lemongrass, similar to scallions in size and appearance but much stiffer, is also usually available at Asian food stores.

To prepare the lemongrass for cooking, trim off the roots and the bottom 2 inches of the stalks. Save the tough tips to use whole in soups. Like bay leaves, they are used for flavoring and are not generally eaten. Slice the remaining center section of the lemongrass into thin rings. These can be bruised to release their flavor by either pounding them in a mortar and pestle or mincing them in a food mill. Use right away. Once cut up, lemongrass loses its flavor quickly.

SERVES 2

½ pound chicken hearts
½ pound chicken livers
½ teaspoon olive oil, divided
½ teaspoon cumin seed
½ teaspoon fennel seed
½ teaspoon coriander seed
6 scallions, greens included, finely chopped
2 cloves garlic, peeled and put through a garlic press
*1 stem lemongrass, sliced and bruised in a mortar and pestle or
  minced in a food mill*
1 teaspoon dark brown sugar
½ teaspoon ground turmeric

Overnight seasoning is needed to bring out the flavors of this dish, so start it the day before you want to serve it.

Rinse the chicken hearts and livers in cold water and gently pat dry with a paper towel, then place them in a Ziploc-type plastic bag and set aside while you put together the seasoning paste for them.

Measure ¼ teaspoon of the olive oil into a small cast-iron skillet or other heavy frying pan and spread it with a spatula to coat the bottom of the pan. Add the cumin, fennel, and coriander seeds and toast over medium heat for 1 to 2 minutes to bring out their flavor.

Transfer the seeds to a mortar and pestle or a small food mill and grind them coarsely. Add the scallions, garlic, lemongrass, and remaining ¼ teaspoon olive oil. Grind again. Once you have a smooth paste, blend in the brown sugar and turmeric.

Place the paste in the bag with the chicken parts and work it gently around the pieces to coat them well. Refrigerate overnight.

About 1½ hours before you want to serve the skewered chicken parts, start a fire in your smoker. While it's preheating, thread the hearts and livers onto bamboo skewers, securing first one liver, then two hearts, one liver, two hearts, and so on.

Place the skewers on the grill, cover the cooker with the lid, and smoke for 1 hour at 210 to 230 degrees F. over wet wood and a pan of hot water.

A sauce or a dip or both can be prepared while the skewers of chicken parts are smoking. If you plan to serve *sambal kecap*, make it up first, as it should steep for a bit to blend the flavors.

SATAY SAUCE

This is the traditional satay sauce — or I should say one version of it, since there are so very many. Based on peanuts, it's nonetheless a far cry from peanut butter. Incidentally, this sauce goes nicely with other skewered fare such as chicken or beef.

MAKES ABOUT 2½ CUPS

> 1 cup shelled unsalted roasted peanuts
> 3 tablespoons peanut oil
> 3 scallions, greens included, chopped
> 2 cloves garlic
> 2 teaspoons grated fresh gingerroot
> ½ cup concentrated chicken stock or 1 chicken bouillon cube dissolved in ½ cup boiling water
> ½ cup rice vinegar
> 3 tablespoons chili powder
> 2 tablespoons dark brown sugar
> 2 tablespoons soy sauce
> 2 tablespoons lime juice
> 2 tablespoons chopped fresh cilantro
> 1 tablespoon tamarind paste

Grind the peanuts briefly in a food mill, taking care not to reduce them to a mush, for then the sauce wouldn't have the right consistency. Set aside.

Measure the oil into a stainless steel or flameproof ceramic saucepan and place it over medium heat. Add the scallions, garlic, and ginger. Sauté just long enough to soften, not brown.

Add the chicken stock or bouillon to the pan and bring to a simmer. Then add the ground peanuts, vinegar, chili powder, brown sugar, soy sauce, lime juice, cilantro, and tamarind paste. Stir to dissolve any clumps of spices or sugar and simmer over reduced heat for 5 to 10 minutes, or until thickened.

Serve warm with the skewered chicken hearts and livers. Any sauce left over can be covered tightly and refrigerated for later use. Thus protected, satay sauce will keep for several weeks.

SAMBAL KECAP

As an alternative to the customary peanut sauce, try this one, more a dip than a sauce, or serve it as an additional condiment for variety.

MAKES A LITTLE MORE THAN ½ CUP

> 1 tablespoon peanut oil
> ½ small onion, finely chopped
> 1 tablespoon tamarind paste
> 1 fresh chili pepper, stemmed, seeded, and minced
> 3 cloves garlic, peeled and put through a garlic press
> 3 tablespoons soy sauce
> 3 tablespoons lemon juice
> 2 tablespoons hot water

Measure the oil into a small stainless steel or flameproof ceramic saucepan and place it over low heat. Add the onion and sauté until soft and transparent. Remove from the heat and blend in the tamarind paste. Then stir in the chili pepper, garlic, soy sauce, lemon juice, and water. Let steep for 1 hour.

Serve at room temperature.

VEGEBOBS

Many a campsite and cookout fire in my youth was littered with vegetables from a shish kebab. It wasn't that I didn't like vegetables, merely that in the fifties one alternated chunks of meat, tomatoes, peppers, mushrooms, and onions on a skewer and roasted the whole kit and caboodle over the fire. First the tomatoes would fall off. Next the mushrooms would dry out, split, and fall off. Eventually, the peppers would hit the flames, and by the time the meat was done, maybe a piece of onion or two would still be clinging to the skewer to go with the meat.

I have no idea why it took so long to come up with the notion of separate skewers for the different types of fare so each could cook at its own pace. I suspect the delay had to do with the fact that a shish kebab was supposed to have everything on one skewer, and back then we did the shish kebab the way it was supposed to be done. Of course, that was then and this is now, as the contemporary saying goes. Now a lot of people skip the meat entirely and have vegebobs.

Here, then, is a perfect accompaniment to the other kabobs in this chapter. Tuck a few vegebobs on the grill along with your skewers of seafood, chicken, or beef, and you'll have a well-rounded smoked meal. Besides, smoked vegebobs are delicious.

Okra is optional. Okra is always optional in my book. However, I should add that, smoked, this vegetable isn't the slimy, slippery stuff most of us northerners visualize as we politely decline our helping.

SERVES 4

12 large cherry tomatoes
12 medium-size okra pods
12 shiitake mushrooms
4 yellow bell peppers
2 baby zucchini
¼ cup olive oil
¼ cup cider vinegar
1 clove garlic, peeled and put through a garlic press
1 tablespoon finely chopped fresh mint
1 teaspoon finely chopped fresh thyme

About 2 hours before you want these veggie kabobs to be ready, rinse the vegetables and pat dry. If you have a bunch of tomatoes to choose from, select your dozen from those with skins intact if at all possible. Split skins make for loss of valuable juice.

Trim off the stem and bottom end of each of the okra pods and stem the mushrooms as well. Cut the peppers into squares measuring about 2 inches across. Trim the ends from the zucchini, slice it into sections about 2 inches long, then quarter these sections lengthwise so you'll be able to push the skewer through the peel of each piece, to help secure the squash as it softens in cooking.

Thread the vegetables onto bamboo skewers, alternating the different pieces as pleases your eye. Fit them loosely on the skewers to give the cooking smoke room to penetrate them. Lay the veggie-laden skewers on a large platter or piece of aluminum foil and set aside.

In a small mixing bowl, combine the olive oil, vinegar, garlic, mint, and thyme. Dribble some of this marinade over the skewered vegetables and let rest for 1 hour. Reserve the extra marinade.

If the only thing on the agenda for your smoker is cooking the veggie kabobs, start a fire in the fire pan when the vegetables have been marinating for about 30 minutes. Add wet wood to the coals and hot water to the water pan just before putting the kabobs on the grill.

Smoke the kabobs in the snugly lidded cooker at 220 to 240 degrees F. for 30 minutes, or longer if needed, basting with the reserved marinade every 15 minutes.

11. VEGETABLES ARE FOR SMOKING, TOO

To a true-blue, dyed-in-the-wool pit master, the thought of putting potatoes, onions, or corn in there with the real stuff can only be counted a heresy. But what a tasty heresy.

In deference to said pit master, I must admit that to smoke or not to smoke is a question I often ask myself about vegetables. Like anything else, smoke cooking can be overdone, so the matter becomes one of what's actually to be gained by it here. A smoky flavor is not among the first answers to come to mind.

Considering the high moisture content of vegetables — most of them are, after all, 90 percent water — the attempt to impart a smoky taste might seem rather like trying to smoke-cure soup. Then too, compared with meats, most vegetables cook rather quickly and thus have less time to absorb the fragrance from smoldering wood.

What's gained by smoke-cooking vegetables, on the other hand, is convenience — without its usual concomitant loss of flavor. While smoked vegetables may retain only a hint of the woodsy scents surrounding them in the cooker, they are every bit as luscious as their more conventionally prepared counterparts, if not more so, and it's far easier to tuck a few stuffed tomatoes on the grill next to a nearly done pork roast than it is to haul out a separate pan and bake them in the oven. It also makes for a much cooler kitchen on hot summer days. The same holds true for corn on the cob, normally requiring that enormous kettle of boiling water.

Then, too, there are vegetarians, of which our older daughter, Genevieve, is one. Being able to smoke vegetables along with dishes for carnivores permits both camps to join in the fun of a barbecue. The truth of the matter is that smoke-cooked vegetables need not be bland substitutes for "the real thing," but are delicious in their own right. Many a time, I've seen nonvegetarians choose a portabella burger, for instance, over a regular one.

PORTABELLA BURGERS

Think of a cookout, and what comes to most people's mind is a succulent steak or a juicy hamburger or, better yet, a cheeseburger entirely enveloped in well-melted cheese. However, where there's a vegetarian in the family, as in ours, one's perspective changes. For both those who have forsworn meat and those pursuing novel alternatives to it, there's a most savory burger waiting to be tried, portabella. Besides being delectable, it's lighter fare than a heavy hamburger, much less conducive to that groggy postprandial craving for a nap.

As to the roll to put the burger on, normally I'll choose a crisply crusted one over the soft variety, a rare exception to this preference being the bun for a portabella. Maybe because of the mushroom's own softness, maybe because of its remarkable juiciness when smoked, this treat seems to need the soft touch. Fresh basil leaves crown the whole mouthwatering affair.

SERVES 4

> 4 portabella mushrooms about 3½ inches in diameter
> ½ cup olive oil
> ¼ cup balsamic vinegar
> 2 cloves garlic, peeled and put through a garlic press
> 4 pats butter, about 1 tablespoon total
> 4 fresh soft onion rolls
> 12 large fresh basil leaves

Start a fire in your smoker first thing, about 1½ hours before the burger call. Build up a good bed of coals and put hot water in the water pan.

Rinse the mushrooms if necessary, pat dry, then cut the stem off each one flush with the cap.

Pour the olive oil into a small measuring cup, add the vinegar and garlic, and whisk together until well mixed.

Place the mushrooms, stem side up, on the smoker grill. Slowly pour one-quarter of the oil and vinegar mix into each fluted mushroom cap, circling the stem. Dot the stems with a pat of butter and put the cooker's lid on.

Smoke the portabellas for 1 hour at 200 to 220 degrees F. They will be deep golden, tender, and fragrant.

To serve, place each portabella, stem side up, on the bottom half of a soft onion roll, lay 3 basil leaves over it, and cover with the onion-flecked top half of the roll.

GARLIC BOMBS

Garlic has risen from obscurity to the status of a favorite American flavoring over the past couple of decades. Even so, the garlic bulb served whole is as yet a rarity, an esoteric appetizer appearing occasionally on select restaurant menus. Garlic cookers are beginning to appear in kitchen catalogs, though, and the herb is gaining acceptance as a vegetable — healthy and tasty, too. People are discovering that, cooked long and gently, garlic bulbs yield a rich, buttery cream that's delightful spread on bread, used like mayonnaise and mustard to accent other foods, or simply eaten plain. They make a great nibble to serve while a main course is being readied for the table.

SERVES 6 AS AN APPETIZER OR A SIDE DISH

6 large whole bulbs garlic
2 teaspoons salt
¼ cup olive oil

If the garlic bulbs are to be served as an appetizer or an accompaniment to a main dish already being smoked, they need only be tucked in around whatever else you're cooking on the grill some-where between 4 and 6 hours before dinnertime, assuming the smoker is working away at 210 to 230 degrees F. If, on the other hand, nothing else is on the smoker's agenda for the day, you'll need to preheat it to that temperature, again some 4 to 6 hours before you plan to serve the bulbs.

To prepare the bulbs for smoking, slice off the tip of each and gently peel away the papery skin encasing the cloves, leaving the base to hold them together and keep the bulb intact.

Fill a small saucepan partway with cold water, shake in the salt, and add the garlic bulbs, making sure there's enough liquid to cover them. Bring to a boil and simmer for 2 minutes, then lift the bulbs out of the pan with a slotted spoon.

Pour the olive oil into a small bowl, add the bulbs, and swish them around in the oil until they're well coated.

Transfer the bulbs to the grill, put the lid on your cooker, and smoke for 4 to 6 hours at 210 to 230 degrees F. over wet wood and a pan of hot water and beneath a tightly fitted grill cover.

For an appetizer, serve the garlic bulbs with hunks of good coun-try bread. To complement a main course, nestle them next to a not-too-spicy entrée, say a delicately spiced fish, whose flavor will not overpower the surprisingly smooth, light taste of the garlic. The bulbs are also grand served in solitary splendor, hot and fragrant from the smoker. To eat them, simply separate the cloves and squeeze out the soft, buttery insides.

EMBER ONIONS

N o barbecue is complete, surely, without some sweet cooked onions. However, the form this cooking should take is a matter of considerable debate, essentially focused on the question of how dainty the dining is to be.

In my opinion, no doubt nurtured by years around the campfire, there's nothing quite like a steaming, finger-burning onion pulled from deep within the fire and charred totally black on the outside. Magnificent, absolutely. Messy too, no doubt about it. By today's campcraft standards — keyed to a milieu in which outdoorsy vacationing has become synonymous with wheeled living rooms only slightly smaller than a 747, in which the absence of cable television is a major deprivation — such a messy morsel is as passé as a tent.

Enter aluminum foil, the chef's version of duct tape, by now the well-nigh indispensable outdoor-cooking tool. Foil-wrapped veggies emerge from the fire far less disheveled than their unwrapped counterparts, and while I admit the benefit grudgingly, they permit a variety in flavoring of which the ember-roasted onion is simply not capable. Take your pick — or make some of both and let diners choose between them.

SERVES 1 — MULTIPLY BY THE NUMBER OF PERSONS TO BE SERVED

1 large sweet onion

FOR THE FOIL-WRAPPED VERSION ONLY
1 teaspoon balsamic vinegar
1 clove garlic, slivered
a few pinches of sugar
a few pinches of dried oregano
a few pinches of ground black pepper
a few pinches of salt
1 teaspoon butter

Plan on about 1½ hours' preparation time for the ember-roasted onion. Rinse and place the onion in a bowl of cold water to cover and weight with a small plate to make sure it's completely submerged. Soak for 1 hour.

Assuming you're cooking other things in the smoker and thus it's already hot and steaming, push the coals in the fire pan aside and set the onion right on the embers. Cover with the coals you just moved. Leave to roast, undisturbed, for 30 minutes before rummaging around in the coals to find it.

To serve, spear the onion with a fork and split it down the middle from tip to stem end with a sharp knife. Trim off enough of the bottom so that the onion layers break free. Squeeze out the tender insides, leaving the charred shell behind.

For the foil-wrapped rendition, first peel the vegetable and slice it thinly crosswise. Place the first slice on a piece of aluminum foil large enough to be folded around the whole onion once it's re-assembled. Sprinkle the slice with a little balsamic vinegar, a few of the garlic slivers, and a pinch each of the sugar, oregano, pepper, and salt. Anchor the seasoning with a thin pat of butter. Place the next onion slice on top of the first and repeat. Add the rest of the slices in like fashion, ending with the last little one as a lid to the whole affair. Fold the foil over the onion, making a tight package of it, and seal.

Place the onion packet on the coals in your smoker's fire pan for 20 to 30 minutes. Watch your fingers when you pull it out. The foil will cool quickly, but the onion will remain hot. Don't be fooled by the temperature of the foil, or you'll be licking your fingertips for more reasons than simply to get the very last of the delicious flavor off.

SAUCED POTATOES

In outdoor cookery, potatoes, like onions, are often roasted in their skins right in the coals. I won't go into the pros and cons of that one except to point out that the onion cooked in coals is skinned on serving and the potato is not. Being fond of potato skins, I'm loath to forgo them, but the gritty ash in which a potato excavated from the embers comes coated sets my teeth on edge. Smoked potatoes, on the other hand, set my taste buds on anticipatory edge.

In choosing the seasoning for smoked potatoes, consider what would contrast nicely with your main dish. Spicy ribs, for instance, are complemented by potatoes flavored with a sweet sauce. Mild, sweet meats go well with spicy potatoes.

SERVES 1 — MULTIPLY BY THE NUMBER OF PERSONS TO BE SERVED

1 medium-size baking potato
a barbecue sauce of your choosing

Assuming that the potato is a side dish, that the steam's already up in your smoker, and that you have an appropriate barbecue sauce on hand (the chapter on sauces will give you some ideas), you needn't turn your attention to the spud until about 1 hour before dinnertime.

Scrub the potato, halve it lengthwise, and crosshatch the open face to a depth of about ¼ inch. Brush the hatching liberally with the barbecue sauce.

Smoke at 220 to 240 degrees F. for 30 minutes to 1 hour. Potatoes vary a lot in cooking time depending on their moisture content, so you'll have to prick yours with a fork to check for doneness. While you're pricking, baste with more sauce for extra flavor.

CORN IN THE HUSK

If there's one vegetable that typifies country living, it's sweet corn. To say that corn should go from stalk to pot within no more than 10 minutes, as I've always maintained, is perhaps to overstate the case. But certainly corn not cooked the same day it's harvested is chicken feed. I'm not quite sure why pick-your-own cornfields haven't evolved in the wake of pick-your-own strawberry and blueberry farms, not to mention apple orchards. Maybe someday they will.

Meanwhile, for corn as it was meant to taste, if you can't grow your own, then farm stands and the pickup trucks that sprout like mushrooms along country byways in July and August are the only way to go. Also, once you get the ears home, have dinner early if you must, but cook the corn as soon as you possibly can. In peak season, our family has been known to have just corn for dinner.

SERVES 1 — MULTIPLY BY THE NUMBER OF PERSONS TO BE SERVED

2 ears of corn
butter for slathering on the cob
salt to taste

To prepare an ear of corn for smoking, first pull the husk back gently all the way to the stalk. With luck, it will stay attached at the bottom. If it doesn't, don't give up on that ear, just save the stripped husk. Draw out and discard the silk enveloping the kernels.

Run a bar of butter up and down the corn until all the kernels are well coated. Then pull the husk back up around the ear and tie it together at the opened end. If you inadvertently husked the corn completely, simply wrap the ear in the various pieces of its former sheath and wind the string around it from one end to the other.

Normally, I use only untreated cotton cord for cooking purposes. In this instance, however, what I'm securing is an inedible outer husk, so I like to use bright red or blue, a small but festive adornment that makes the corn seem almost like a gift-wrapped present. When you think about it, that's what it is, considering nature provides us with the treat in its rightful form only a few weeks out of the year.

Place the rewrapped corn on the rack of your smoker over a bit of wet wood and a pan of hot water and cook, covered, at 210 to

230 degrees F. for 20 to 30 minutes. Let me hasten to assure you that I would never, ever boil corn on the cob longer than 2 minutes. I'm not one to overcook this vegetable. But when it's steamed in its husk with only the kernels' own juices and a little butter and salt, the operative heat conductivity is much lower. Hence the extra time. I can assure you that the result will be some of the sweetest, most tender corn you've ever eaten.

Serve in the husk with more butter and salt close at hand to add at the very last minute before feasting.

TOMATOES GORGONZOLA

Like corn, tomatoes are an eagerly anticipated once-a-year seasonal treat in our family. Come the first or second week of August, the Sweet 100s are ripening, racemes of the bright, cheerful fruit cascading from each plant. A few weeks later, the beefsteaks are weighing in at a couple of pounds of juiciness apiece, and I'll stand in the garden eating them out of hand like apples. Then the early October frost brings the festival to a close but for a dozen or so rescued underripe tomatoes gathering flavor and the occasional fruit fly on the kitchen bay window sill.

The abundance of the harvest coinciding as it does with the season when pondside smoke cooking is our preferred means of putting dinner on the table, it's not surprising that I often tuck a stuffed tomato or two in the smoker along with whatever fish or meat is cooking there.

SERVES 1 — MULTIPLY BY THE NUMBER OF PERSONS TO BE SERVED

1 large fresh, ripe tomato
4 fresh basil leaves
2 to 3 tablespoons Gorgonzola cheese
1 tablespoon olive oil

If you're going to serve the stuffed tomatoes solo for a summery supper — not a bad idea at all, I might add — and the smoker's not already going strong, start a fire in it about 1 hour beforehand, settle the coals, and add wet wood and a pan of hot water.

Rinse the tomato and partially core it, cutting a circle about ¾ to

1 inch in diameter around the stem end but taking care that the knife doesn't slip all the way through to the bottom of the fruit. You want a crater, not a tunnel.

Line the hole with the basil leaves, then fill to the top with Gorgonzola cheese. Dribble the olive oil over the cheese and the surrounding top of the tomato. Set the cooker's lid on firmly.

Smoke the tomato at 210 to 230 degrees F. for 30 minutes, or until the skin just begins to crack from all that pent-up juiciness inside.

SMOKED BROCCOLI PARMIGIANA

Broccoli is accorded little respect in this country. The butt of presidential jokes and children's tantrums, its production honed to the point where it's more readily available year-round than almost anything besides potatoes and onions, this vegetable has become to the American diet what cabbage is to the Russian one. It is, in short, inevitable.

Yet, all things considered, broccoli can be an amazingly tasty vegetable. Furthermore, like cabbage, it transports and stores well. When you buy broccoli, you want it fresh enough to be crisp, but that's about all you need ask.

SERVES 3 TO 4

> 1 to 1½ pounds broccoli
> ½ cup olive oil
> ¼ cup cider vinegar
> ¼ teaspoon ground white pepper
> dash of salt
> 1 cup freshly grated Parmesan cheese

Rinse the broccoli well and trim the leaf stems and bumps from the stalks. Cut each stalk in half lengthwise, slicing right through the florets at the top, then carve a shallow, wide, V-shaped groove down the center of the stem portion. Set the broccoli aside while you make the marinade.

Pour the oil and vinegar into a shallow pan and add the white pepper and salt. Whisk these ingredients until well blended, then swirl the broccoli in the pan with a fork until it's well covered on all sides with the liquid. Let the broccoli marinate while you start a fire in your smoker — unless the cooker is already hot and working on a main dish.

Once you have coals glowing and some wet wood smoldering in the fire pan, fill the water pan halfway with hot water and turn your attention again to the broccoli. Add the Parmesan cheese to the marinade and swish the broccoli around in it once more.

Place the stalks on the grill with the flat cut sides up. Brush with the remaining marinade, filling the channels in the stems well. Cover the cooker and smoke at 210 to 230 degrees F. for 20 to 30 minutes, or until just tender.

EGGPLANT ANCHOÏADE

The answer of last resort to the pizza-order question "What do you want on it?" is, in my experience, "Anything but anchovies." For most people, eggplant occupies a position in the plant kingdom about as unenviable as that of the little fishes in the seafood realm. This hierarchy of comestibles notwithstanding, Provençals somehow manage to combine the two spurned victuals and effect thereby a most savory delight that we came upon in a small restaurant in Sommières.

Eggplant destined for the smoker must be salted and then dried off if it's not to be too soft and soggy to hold together on the grill. Recipes for this vegetable traditionally call for slicing it, sprinkling the rounds with salt, and then putting them in a colander to drain. I've read those instructions in at least a hundred different places and always follow them myself, mystified, since somehow nothing ever seems to drain out of them by this means.

If, however, I firmly pat the slices dry after they've sat for a while with the salt permeating them, I find I can remove a lot of moisture, drawn out by the salt. Patting them dry intensifies the flavor of the eggplant as well.

1 medium-size eggplant, about 1½ to 2 pounds
salt
¾ cup olive oil, divided
2 tablespoons balsamic vinegar
¼ cup chopped fresh parsley
10 anchovy fillets packed in oil
6 cloves garlic
6 large fresh basil leaves
½ teaspoon ground black pepper
1 egg yolk

Unless your smoker is already in use, start a fire in the fire pan first thing, about 1 hour before dinnertime, so it will be ready when the eggplant is.

Rinse the eggplant and cut it into slices about 1½ inches thick. Salt the slices well and set aside in a colander (if yours actually drains in a colander, please let me know) while you prepare the marinade.

Pour about half of the olive oil into a blender or food processor, followed by the vinegar. Add the parsley, anchovies, garlic, basil, and pepper. Blend these ingredients to a smooth paste.

Heat the remaining olive oil in a small stainless steel or flame-proof ceramic saucepan. Add the anchovy paste, using a spatula if need be to extract the last bit of it from the blender or processor, and stir the mixture over low heat until smooth.

In a small bowl, whip the egg yolk until light. Add it to the anchovy sauce in a slow stream, stirring constantly. Remove from the heat as soon as the sauce has thickened.

Put some wet wood in with the coals in your smoker's fire pan and fill the water pan halfway with hot water. Brush the eggplant with olive oil and place the slices on the grill. If you like your eggplant very tender, set one grill crosswise atop another to support the slices. If you like your eggplant very, very soft, cover the grill partially — not completely, for you don't want to block the flow of moisture and smoke around the cooking vegetable — with heavy-duty aluminum foil. Brush the foil with olive oil and place the eggplant on that.

Spread each slice with some of the anchovy sauce, put the lid on the cooker, and smoke at 210 to 230 degrees F. for 20 to 30 minutes, the specific time depending mostly on how tender you like your eggplant.

SIMPLE CAESAR ZUCCHINI, OR YET ANOTHER ZUCCHINI RECIPE

Zucchini and the summer barbecue season come hand in hand, and considering the vegetable's "I came, I saw, I conquered" attitude in the garden, it's fortunate that it smokes well. Because of its overabundance, zucchini is not a crop that collects many accolades or fancy recipes, and this one is no exception. Then again, who says life can't be simple sometimes?

SERVES 1 — MULTIPLY BY THE NUMBER OF PERSONS TO BE SERVED

1 baby zucchini
your favorite bottled Caesar salad dressing

Assuming the zucchini is to be served with more substantial fare already cooking in the smoker, the only advance preparation needed for this dish is that devoted to the vegetable itself. Plan on marinating it for about 2 hours before it is to be smoked.

Rinse the zucchini, cut it into 4-inch lengths, then slice the lengths into strips about ½ inch wide. Slice the strips in turn into sticks, each again about ½ inch wide.

Lay the sticks no more than two deep in a shallow dish. Pour some of the dressing over them, turning the pieces to coat all sides. Use enough dressing to ensure that all the zucchini pieces are well coated. Set aside to marinate for 1 hour, then turn the sticks and steep for 1 more hour.

Smoke at 210 to 230 degrees F. for about 20 minutes, or until tender and fragrant.

12. TO SAUCE OR NOT TO SAUCE

When, fresh out of college, I began my rendition of the proverbial starving-young-writer career moonlighting as a busboy in a cheap New York City steak house, what startled me most about the establishment was the number of customers who would order the restaurant's top-of-the-line sirloin and then cover it lavishly from bone to fat rim with steak sauce. Why would anyone want to do that to a steak? I asked myself.

In search of an answer to that question, I one day tried the combination. Much to my surprise, having grown up in a family where a light sprinkling of pepper was considered the maximum spicing for a steak, I enjoyed it. All the same, I decided, a steak with steak sauce was an affair entirely different from a steak-steak.

So it is with barbecues. For some people, if there's a sauce, it's a barbecue. If not, well, then it's just plain fare. Other folks feel that if a selection isn't tasty enough as it comes from the grill, without further embellishment, it doesn't deserve to be called a barbecue.

I'm not about to put myself in the middle of that one. Besides, settling the dispute, could it even be done, would silence only the second-most-lively topic of conversation around the smoker. The first — what's the best barbecue sauce of all? — would continue. Even confined as it is to those who do indeed believe the sauce makes the barbecue, that question is akin to determining the best fishing lure of them all, a matter I could debate endlessly with just myself, let alone anyone else.

If whether or not to sauce at all is a matter of controversy, then the right sauce is, among savants on the subject, a matter of religion. Hoarded recipes and inviolate dressings not to be profaned abound. Every barbecue enthusiast champions some consummate accompaniment dear to the heart.

In due time, you'll no doubt discover your own one and only as well. What follows is a sampling of sauces easily rustled up in the kitchen to launch your quest. In addition to this selection, there's also the endless search approach. At the back of the book is a directory of suppliers offering ready-made condiments in enough variety to keep you barbecuing well into the next century without ever serving the same sauce twice.

THE BASIC B SAUCE

M any a pit master's so-called special sauce is a commercial product with one or two secret ingredients added to it. Here's a basic barbecue sauce that's good on almost everything as is but that can also easily become your own special sauce by the addition of one or two secret ingredients.

MAKES A LITTLE MORE THAN 2 CUPS

2 tablespoons butter
1 tablespoon peanut oil
1 medium-size onion, minced
4 cloves garlic, peeled and put through a garlic press
1 tablespoon dry mustard
1 tablespoon ground black pepper
1 tablespoon ground cayenne pepper
1 teaspoon ground cumin
1 cup firmly packed dark brown sugar
½ cup water
2 cups catsup
½ cup cider vinegar
2 tablespoons Worcestershire sauce

Melt the butter and oil in a medium-size stainless steel or flame-proof ceramic saucepan set over low heat. Add the onion and sauté until just translucent. Then add the garlic, dry mustard, black and cayenne peppers, and cumin. Stir to a rough paste, mashing out any obvious lumps. Mix in the brown sugar, followed by the water to help dissolve it smoothly. Add the catsup, vinegar, and Worcestershire sauce and blend well.

Simmer over low heat for about 15 to 20 minutes, stirring occasionally. The thickness of the sauce can be adjusted to your liking by simmering for a shorter or longer time. If it becomes too thick by mistake, simply thin it with water.

ZYDECO ZIP

Louisiana is the home of Tabasco and a thousand other peppery condiments. Counterpointing the capsicum's spicy flavor in Creole cooking are the softer touches of sage and thyme — all the different seasonings orchestrated into the distinctive piquancy of that fare, as invigorating as the zydeco bands of the region. Here's a Creole sauce altogether as zippy as the music.

MAKES ABOUT 2 CUPS

3 tablespoons olive oil
1 medium-size green bell pepper, finely chopped
1 medium-size yellow bell pepper, finely chopped
6 okra pods, stem end removed, seeded and finely chopped
6 cloves garlic, peeled and put through a garlic press
2 teaspoons chili powder
1 teaspoon ground sage
1 teaspoon ground thyme
1 teaspoon coarsely ground black pepper
1 teaspoon ground cayenne pepper
½ teaspoon ground white pepper
½ teaspoon salt
1 sixteen-ounce can crushed tomatoes
½ cup red wine vinegar
¼ cup lemon juice
¼ cup prepared hot mustard
2 teaspoons Tabasco or similar hot red pepper sauce

Warm the olive oil in a medium-size stainless steel or flameproof ceramic saucepan set over low heat. Add the green and yellow bell peppers, okra, and garlic. Sauté until soft. Stir in the chili powder; sage; thyme; black, cayenne, and white peppers; and salt, mixing well to disperse any clumps. Blend in the tomatoes, vinegar, lemon juice, mustard, and Tabasco or other hot red pepper sauce.

Simmer for 30 minutes, or until as thick as you like it. Serve warm to add some zip to your smoke cookery.

COCA-Q SAUCE

C oca-Cola is a cooking ingredient down Atlanta way. Considering the soda's Georgia origin, this instance of folk enthusiasm should come as no surprise. What might is that a barbecue sauce incorporating the drink actually tastes good.

Initially, Coke syrup formed the base for this sauce. However, Coke syrup has gone the way of the soda fountain whose mainstay it once was. So here's a formulation using the beverage itself.

MAKES ABOUT 1½ CUPS

2 tablespoons butter
6 scallions, greens included, chopped
4 cloves garlic, peeled and minced
1 six-ounce can tomato paste
¾ cup dark corn syrup
¾ cup Coca-Cola
¼ cup cider vinegar
2 tablespoons Worcestershire sauce
1 tablespoon Tabasco or similar hot red pepper sauce

Melt the butter in a small stainless steel or flameproof ceramic saucepan set over low heat. Add the scallions and garlic and cook for 2 to 3 minutes, or until the green pieces of scallion are well wilted. Stir in the tomato paste, followed by the corn syrup, Coca-Cola, vinegar, Worcestershire sauce, and Tabasco or other hot red pepper sauce.

Blend well and simmer, uncovered and stirring occasionally, for 30 minutes or until pleasantly thick.

TEXAS TAR

Most traditional barbecue sauces have a distinct dark red tinge to them, betraying the tomato base they share. The more recent fruit-based additions to the repertoire of barbecue condiments tend to be clearer and lighter in color. Here, however, is a fruit sauce as black as the gushers that made its home state wealthy. Lekvar, by the way, is a prune butter sometimes used as a pastry filling.

MAKES ABOUT 3 CUPS

> 3 tablespoons butter
> 6 cloves garlic, peeled and minced
> 1 tablespoon coarsely ground black pepper
> ½ teaspoon ground mace
> 1 cup Worcestershire sauce
> 1 cup red wine vinegar
> 1 cup lekvar
> ¼ cup molasses

In a medium-size stainless steel or flameproof ceramic saucepan, melt the butter and sauté the garlic until golden. Whisk in the pepper and mace, then add the Worcestershire sauce, vinegar, lekvar, and molasses. Blend well and simmer for 5 minutes.

Don't wait for this sauce to really thicken, for it never will. Like Texas tar in the summertime, this is a thin, hot sauce that spills its flavor over the meat. Serve straight from the stove in a warmed pitcher or sauceboat.

PEACHES 'N' CREAM

Many a good barbecue sauce is based on fruit nowadays. Since in fact, botanically speaking, a tomato is a fruit, I suppose one could argue that fruit is the most common constituent of any barbecue sauce. Still, one based on peaches might seem to be asking a lot of taste buds primed to mediate the hot, spicy flavors of a grill. In actuality, it provides a soothing contrast to them.

MAKES ABOUT 2½ CUPS

2 tablespoons butter
1 small onion, minced
2 tablespoons dark brown sugar
1 teaspoon ground cloves
1 teaspoon ground cayenne pepper
1 sixteen-ounce can sliced peaches in heavy syrup
½ cup Bailey's Irish Cream
½ cup chopped bread-and-butter pickles

Melt the butter in a small stainless steel or flameproof ceramic saucepan set over low heat, add the onion, and sauté until golden. Stir in the brown sugar, cloves, and cayenne pepper, mixing well. Drain the peaches, reserving the syrup. Cut the slices in half and add them to the saucepan. Lightly blend in first the Bailey's Irish Cream, then the pickles.

Simmer, stirring gently occasionally, for 20 minutes, or until the sauce thickens nicely. Chill before serving.

APPLESAUCE SAUCE

Apples go particularly well with pork, and this sauce perfectly complements pork ribs. The flavor is intensified by the use of both prepared applesauce and fresh apples. Chunky applesauce can be substituted for the diced raw apples, saving preparation time, but the resulting condiment won't have quite the same luscious apple taste as one made with fresh apples. The tamarind paste, found on the shelves of Asian groceries, adds a unique tang to the apple flavor.

MAKES ABOUT 4 CUPS

⅓ cup butter, divided
½ medium-size red onion, minced
2 cups diced unpeeled apples, preferably Granny Smith or similar tart variety, or 1¼ cups chunky-style applesauce
2 cups puree-style applesauce
1 cup white grape juice
3 tablespoons light corn syrup
2 tablespoons cider vinegar
1 tablespoon tamarind paste
½ teaspoon ground cinnamon
½ teaspoon ground nutmeg

Melt half the butter in a medium-size stainless steel or flameproof ceramic saucepan set over low heat. Add the onion and sauté until soft. Then add the rest of the butter, letting it melt in the heat of the pan, and the diced apples. Toss over low heat just long enough to coat the apples with the butter and onion.

If you're using all applesauce instead of half fresh apples and half applesauce, simply add the extra butter to the hot pan, let it melt, and stir it into the softened onion pieces.

Add the applesauce, grape juice, and corn syrup and stir well. Pour the vinegar into a small cup, dilute the tamarind paste in it, and blend in the cinnamon and nutmeg. Whisk this thinned paste into the other ingredients.

Simmer slowly for 30 minutes, stirring occasionally. Serve hot or cold.

RASPBERRY RIB DIP

Raspberries are in vogue, in everything from desserts to vinegars, so it's not surprising to find them on the barbecue circuit. Old-time raspberry recipes call for freshly stewed berries with the seeds strained out, but seedless preserves do nicely here. Just make sure to use preserves or jam, not jelly, for maximum flavor.

This sauce is particularly good with venison and other game as well as with barbecued pork ribs.

MAKES ABOUT 2 CUPS

1½ cups seedless red or black raspberry preserves
2 tablespoons red raspberry vinegar
2 tablespoons lemon juice
1 teaspoon lemon zest
1 teaspoon Worcestershire sauce
1 teaspoon prepared mustard, preferably Dijon
¼ teaspoon ground mace

Scoop the raspberry preserves into a small stainless steel or flameproof ceramic saucepan and blend in the vinegar, lemon juice and zest, Worcestershire sauce, mustard, and mace. Heat to boiling, then simmer gently for 5 minutes. Serve hot or cold.

IN-A-PICKLE SAUCE

A ll of France loves a Western, Jerry Lewis, and food served au naturel beneath an arbor in Provence. Of late, such a repast has often leaned toward *le barbecue*, with — for a quintessential French touch, naturally — pickles in the sauce. In France, a sauce so endowed is likely to be found at any well-stocked charcuterie specializing in pork delicacies, not to mention on many kitchen shelves.

Pickles really do go well with smoked pork, but not if the meat is super spicy. This sauce is a lovely, piquant foil for, say, a garlic-accented pork roast, where the smoky flavor predominates.

MAKES ABOUT 3 CUPS

4 tablespoons butter
6 shallots or 4 scallions, greens included, chopped
2 tablespoons flour
¾ cup white wine
¼ cup white vinegar
2½ cups concentrated beef stock or 5 beef bouillon cubes dissolved in 2½ cups boiling water
1 bay leaf, finely ground in a mortar and pestle
2 medium-size tomatoes, diced
1 teaspoon sugar
12 small cornichons or 6 small sour pickles, julienned
½ teaspoon ground thyme
2 teaspoons minced fresh parsley

Melt the butter in a medium-size stainless steel or flameproof ceramic saucepan set over low heat. Add the shallots or scallions and sauté until soft and translucent. Sprinkle in the flour, blend, and cook, stirring, until the mixture is the color of cappuccino. Whisk in the wine, vinegar, and beef stock or bouillon. Add the ground bay leaf and stir.

Let this brown sauce simmer, uncovered, for 30 to 45 minutes, whisking occasionally to keep it from scorching on the bottom of the pan as it is reduced and thickens.

Meanwhile, in a separate small nonreactive pan, combine the

tomatoes and sugar with just enough water to keep them from sticking. Simmer until soft.

When the brown sauce is thick and rich, strain the tomatoes into the larger pan through a sieve, running a wooden spoon lightly back and forth over the pulp to work it through the mesh. Blend the pureed tomatoes into the sauce.

Add the cornichons or sour pickles, thyme, and parsley, stirring gently, just before serving.

JALAPEÑO SAUCE

On the heat scale, jalapeño peppers come in at a measly 5,000 Scovilles — enough for them to be considered snappy, not much more. Now the Scoville scale, especially if the pungency of the capsicums is measured using a laboratory method called liquid chromatography, provides a pretty precise assessment of hotness. However, it doesn't take flavor into account.

Much is made of superhot chilies like the Thai, rated at 50,000 to 100,000 Scovilles, and the placid-looking, yellow-orange Habanero, ranked as high as 300,000 Scovilles. All the same, for most of us mortals, these blistering macho chilies leave no room for taste beyond the fire. One reason I like jalapeños is that they have flavor as well as heat.

Besides their natural flavor, jalapeños especially lend themselves to smoke cooking for a historic reason. Smoke-dried jalapeños were a staple of the Aztec diet. Known then — as, in fact, to the present day — as *chipotle,* from the Aztec words *chil* (chili) and *poctli* (smoked), these peppers were smoke-cured rather than sun-dried because their plumpness precluded the simpler but less thorough sun-drying.

Well-founded tradition and superb flavor — what more could you ask of a sauce?

MAKES ABOUT 2 CUPS

3 tablespoons olive oil
1 medium onion, minced
3 cloves garlic, peeled and minced
1 teaspoon chili powder
1 teaspoon ground coriander
½ cup firmly packed dark brown sugar
1 six-ounce can tomato paste
½ cup concentrated beef stock or 1 beef bouillon cube dissolved
* in ½ cup boiling water*
½ cup red wine
½ cup cider vinegar
2 tablespoons Worcestershire sauce
2 tablespoons minced pickled jalapeño pepper

Measure the olive oil into a small stainless steel or flameproof ceramic saucepan set over low heat. Add the onion and garlic and sauté for 2 to 3 minutes, or until soft. Stir in the chili powder and coriander, then the brown sugar, pressing out any large clumps of spices or sugar with the back of the spoon. Add the tomato paste and blend well. Pour in the beef stock or bouillon, along with the wine and vinegar. Add the Worcestershire sauce and stir until all the ingredients are well blended.

Sprinkle in the jalapeño, bring the sauce to a boil, and simmer for 5 minutes. Serve hot.

MOLE

Visiting Mexico in my youth, I discovered cooking with chocolate. At first, having theretofore associated chocolate strictly with a sweet tooth, I met the idea of hot-and-spicy chocolate fare with considerable consternation. All the same, the subtle blend of chocolate and chili flavoring that infuses the archetypal Mexican mole eventually won me over.

The chili component of this mole is the ancho, the dried form of the poblano pepper. Fresh poblanos are attractive, plump green peppers often stuffed with cheese and meat to make *chiles rellenos.* Dried, they change not only their name, but their color as well. Anchos are a dark mahogany. Between their deep cast and that of the chocolate, this mole is rendered almost black.

In point of fact, mole comes in red, green, brown, and other colors, and the reason for that is very simple. The Spanish word *mole* could almost be translated as "everything but the kitchen sink." Loosely, it means "mixture" or "stew." In the familiar guacamole, for instance, the sauce is a blend of vegetables, albeit one dominated by avocado, or *guaca*. In plain, everyday mole, anything goes.

Mole is often called the national dish of Mexico. Far different from the fajitas and tacos so popular north of the border, its singular renown is well deserved. Traditionally served with turkey and other poultry, mole also makes a fine dipping sauce for pork.

MAKES ABOUT 3 CUPS

3 large ripe tomatoes, quartered (if fresh garden or vegetable-
    stand tomatoes are unavailable, use 1 sixteen-ounce can
    crushed tomatoes, drained)
10 anchos, stemmed and seeded
1 medium onion, chopped
4 cloves garlic, peeled and chopped
1 cup pecans, chopped
½ cup crushed corn taco shells
½ teaspoon ground cloves
½ teaspoon ground coriander
¼ teaspoon ground cinnamon
¼ teaspoon ground cumin
¼ teaspoon ground cayenne pepper
4 tablespoons lard or vegetable shortening
1 cup concentrated chicken stock or 2 chicken bouillon cubes
    dissolved in 1 cup water
2 one-ounce squares unsweetened baking chocolate

In a blender or food processor, combine the tomatoes, anchos, onion, garlic, and pecans. Add the crushed taco shells, followed by the cloves, coriander, cinnamon, cumin, and cayenne pepper. Blend until smooth.

Melt the lard or shortening in a fairly large stainless steel or flameproof ceramic saucepan. Add the puree and heat for 5 minutes, stirring constantly. Slowly pour in the chicken stock or bouillon, still stirring, then add the chocolate squares.

When the chocolate has melted, let the sauce simmer over very low heat for 30 minutes, or until good and thick. Stir frequently, checking regularly that the sauce is not sticking to the bottom of the pan, or the black coloring will be from burning rather than from the chilies and chocolate.

SOURCES FOR BARBECUE SUPPLIES

SAUCES, SPICES, CONDIMENTS, AND COMESTIBLES

Adriana's Caravan
409 Vanderbilt Street
Brooklyn, NY 11218
(800) 316-0820

A sauce supplier, this firm offers, among others, Afri-Q, an Ethiopian-style berberé.

The Baker's Catalogue
P.O. Box 876
Norwich, VT 05055
(800) 827-6836

This source of cooking supplies is primarily for bakers, as its name implies. However, it carries some excellent kitchen tongs, herb choppers, graters, and other items very handy on the barbecue circuit.

Calido Chile Traders
5360 Merriam Drive
Merriam, KS 66203
(800) LOTT-HOT

More salsas, sauces, marinades, and jerks than any palate could possibly survive are available from this source, along with spicy mustards, spicy mushrooms, and spicy peanut butter — yes, peanut butter!

Creamery Brook Bison
19 Purvis Road
Brooklyn, CT 06234
(860) 779-0837

All manner of buffalo meat, from roasts to filet mignon, can be shipped from this supplier to anywhere in the United States.

Flamingo Flats
P.O. Box 441
St. Michaels, MD 21663
(800) HOT-8841

Clients of this firm can choose from more than 300 hot sauces, and for those who can't make up their mind, there's a Hot Sauce of the Month Club.

The Great Barbecue Sauce Catalog
Kirby Enterprises Ltd.
P.O. Box 43357
Baltimore, MD 21236
(800) 6-SAUCES

Famous restaurant sauces from Struttin' Gates, Chowning's Tavern, Pigman's, Bessinger's Piggie Park, and others are available through this mail-order supplier.

The Great Southern Sauce Co.
5705 Kavanaugh
Little Rock, AR 72207
(800) 437-2823

Sauces and rubs galore, including such Arkansas originals as Tips Dry Rub, Razorback, and Stubby's Sauce, can be ordered from this firm.

Mo Hotta — Mo Betta
P.O. Box 4136
San Luis Obispo, CA 93403
(800) 462-3220

Dried chilies, barbecue sauces, salsas, and spicy condiments of every kind, including tamarind, are available from this source, not to mention such novel accompaniments as martini olives stuffed with Thai chilies and jalapeño hot fudge sauce, along with more earthy but often elusive provisions like cassava flour.

EQUIPMENT AND ACCESSORIES

Big John Grills and Rotisseries
P.O. Box 5250
Pleasant Gap, PA 16823
(800) 326-9575

As the name implies, this firm carries a broad range of grills and rotisseries. But, as the name might also imply, they're big, primarily geared to commercial operations.

The Brinkmann Corp.
4215 McEwen Road
Dallas, TX 75244
(800) 468-5252

This manufacturer supplies a full range of silo smokers — charcoal, gas, and electric — along with accessories.

Cabela's
812 Thirteenth Avenue
Sidney, NE 69160
(800) 237-4444

Known primarily for its extensive line of sportsmen's gear, the Cabela catalog also features a good selection of smokers as well as meat-processing equipment for hunters.

Chef's Catalog
3215 Commercial Avenue
Northbrook, IL 60062
(800) 338-3232

Billing itself as a purveyor of "professional restaurant equipment for the home chef," this catalog includes a broad range of useful barbecue accessories, from knives to smoker/grill toppers.

Grill Lover's Catalog
Char-Broil
P.O. Box 1300
Columbus, GA 31902
(706) 571-7000

Highlighting the Char-Broil brand of grills, this catalog also carries just about everything a smoke chef could ever want, from basting guns and slicing tongs to nutshell briquettes.

Jurgens Grill Co.
P.O. Box 45218
Tacoma, WA 98445
(206) 846-1745

This manufacturer supplies a reduced-Btu gas-fired grill especially designed for low-temperature cooking.

Klose Fabrication Inc.
2214½ W. 34th Street
Houston, TX 77018
(713) 686-8720

From family size to 42- by 120-inch two-axle trailers, a full range of barbecue smokers is available from this manufacturer.

Lang Manufacturing Co.
P.O. Box 547
Nahunta, GA 31553
(912) 462-6146

The trailer-mounted, heavy-duty, professional-size drum smokers offered by this supplier feature an offset firebox.

National Barbecue Association
P.O. Box 29051
Charlotte, NC 28229
(704) 531-6441

Primarily a trade association, this organization offers an affiliate membership for $25 that includes a subscription to Barbecue Today *and might well be of interest to the enthusiastic backyard barbecuer.*

Oklahoma Joe's
1616 W. Airport Road
Stillwater, OK 74075
(405) 377-3080

Barrel smokers with an offset firebox are the specialty of this manufacturer, and the models range in size from a 14-inch-grill tailgater to a trailer-mounted model with tandem axles featuring a 3,834-square-inch grill.

Peoples Smoke-N-Grill
75 Mill Street
Cumberland, RI 02864
(800) 729-5800

This firm supplies natural hardwood charcoal and a wide selection of chips, from ash to sweet birch to thyme, as well as accessory smoking equipment such as marinade injectors and a bevy of New England barbecue sauces.

Pioneer Fabricating Co.
1013 Jarvis Road
Fort Worth, TX 76131
(817) 232-4303

Two professional barrel smokers, one 5 feet long, the other 6 feet long, both equipped with all the features, including chrome trim, are available from this firm.

Pitt's and Spitt's
14221 Eastex Freeway
Houston, TX 77032
(800) 521-2947

Supplier of a full line of charcoal and propane smokers, this company also carries an extensive selection of barbecue accessories, from knives to tongs and spatulas to super hot mitts.

Residential's Fireplace and Barb-B-Que
528½ Main Street
Indian Orchard, MA 01151
(413) 543-2257

Essentially a regional retail store, this establishment is one of the few that can get you the Japanese Kamado ceramic smoker.

The Sausagemaker
26 Military Road
Buffalo, NY 14207
(716) 876-5521

For the serious smoke chef desirous of turning out homemade sausages, this firm carries a complete line of equipment, casings, and spices suited to that purpose.

Swisher Mower and Machine
P.O. Box 67
Warrensburg, MD 64093
(800) 222-8183

Several models of a rotisserie smoker available with a unique set of rotating trays and a solar unit for powering the spit are available from this manufacturer.

Traeger Industries
1385 E. College Street
Mount Angel, OR 97362
(503) 845-9234

The specialty of this firm is an auger-fed smoker grill using special wood pellets, also available from the company, as its fuel source.

Weber-Stephen Products Co.
560 S. Hicks Road
Palatine, IL 60067
(800) 446-1071

The classic Weber line of kettle grills is available in various models from this manufacturer.

Willie's Chicken Sitter
Nuñez Enterprises Inc.
P.O. Box 622
Stafford, TX 77477
(713) 261-5523

This is the source for Willie's self-basting ceramic chicken holders, which work wonders for the succulence of fowl.

INDEX